RECIPES
MY
MOTHER
COOKED

RECIPES MY MOTHER COOKED

100 home-cooked recipes from the country's
favourite foodies

Foreword by the McGrath Foundation

Introduction by Kate McGhie

Edited by Philippa Sandall

ALLEN&UNWIN

Allen & Unwin's fundraising appeal with the McGrath Foundation
commenced upon publication of this book, and will continue for the life of the book.

www.mcgrathfoundation.com.au

The photograph on pp. 27 and 117 courtesy of iStockphoto/TPopova
The photograph on pp. 11, 15, 109 and 143 courtesy of iStockphoto/twohumans
The photograph on pp. 51, 81 and 173 courtesy of iStockphoto/WitR
The photograph on pp. 9, 75 and 131 courtesy of iStockphoto/Jabiru
The photograph on pp. 5, 69 and 103 courtesy of iStockphoto/qingwa
The photograph on p. 182 is by photographer Peter Mack.
Some border images taken from *Japanese Patterns*, published by The Pepin Press, www.pepinpress.com
Thanks to Dover Publications/Floral Design 2004 for the use of patterns throughout.

First published in 2010

Allen & Unwin
83 Alexander Street
Crows Nest NSW 2065
Australia
Phone: (61 2) 8425 0100
Fax: (61 2) 9906 2218
Email: info@allenandunwin.com
Web: www.allenandunwin.com

Cataloguing-in-Publication details are available
from the National Library of Australia
www.librariesaustralia.nla.gov.au

ISBN 978 1 74237 331 7

Design by Marylouise Brammer
Index by Puddingburn
Set in 10.5/13 pt Rockwell Light by Bookhouse, Sydney
Printed in Australia by Ligare Pty Ltd, Sydney

10 9 8 7 6 5 4 3 2 1

Contents

Foreword by the McGrath Foundation

It never ceases to amaze me that something as simple as a glimpse, a touch, a vague smell on a breeze or the taste of something familiar can immediately transport you to a time 'once before', which was usually enjoyed with family or friends and so strongly associated with a period of happiness or security.

For a lot of people associated with the McGrath Foundation it is moments like these that we hold on to—the ones that make us smile and laugh, and that we enjoy sharing with new friends we meet along the way.

And so when Allen & Unwin approached the McGrath Foundation about becoming partners on this project we jumped at the chance—not only because we were as keen as anyone else to learn the hidden family recipes of some of our best-loved Australians, but also because we know the importance of holding on to these memories and ensuring they are passed on to the next generation. After all, this is how we honour our loved ones, how we testify to their lives and how we build and sustain traditions that they themselves were once part of.

Jane's very personal experience with breast cancer, and her shared story, fundamentally shaped the McGrath Foundation's key purposes: to increase the number of breast care nurses across Australia while at the same time increasing breast awareness among younger women.

Jane and Glenn knew firsthand the amazing impact that access to a breast care nurse can have on both a woman experiencing breast cancer and on her family. The relief the breast care nurse provides, just by being there to listen or make a cup of tea, and their ability to make what seems at times an overwhelming experience almost bearable, leave most people in awe of their capacity to give. No doubt there have also been many tried and trusted recipes exchanged along the way to try and make life that little bit easier for someone not feeling well, or a husband or friend struggling to find something the kids will eat!

To Allen & Unwin, thank you for initiating this project—it is such a lovely way for people to pull together and share their stories. To everyone who contributed, thank you for becoming part of the McGrath Foundation family—we couldn't be prouder to know you all. And to you who have bought this book, thank you. From Jane's simple idea we've grown our ambition: we are now striving for a future in which every Australian family affected by breast cancer has access to a breast care nurse. In your decision to buy this book you've helped us get one step closer to that dream.

Always remember that together we can make a difference.

Kylea Tink
Managing Director, McGrath Foundation
Mum to three, daughter to two, sister to three, wife to one,
and friend to those I love

Introduction by Kate McGhie

Recipes have a language all their own. They evoke a range of emotions—from nostalgia to unbridled joy. They connect us to tangible moments in time, to delicious tastes, occasional kitchen disasters and favourite family get-togethers.

But a family recipe is also a family history. Along with my mother's valuable cooking tutelage I also inherited her cookbooks, full of well-tested and exquisitely handwritten recipes passed down through the generations. Their pages, bearing traces of past ingredients and generations of busy hands, include recipes from neighbours and friends with personalised grading systems noted alongside. Even today, I would not dare alter those recipes honoured with a bold tick alongside for fear of Nanna's wrath reaching me from beyond. However, recipes evolve. As they are passed along they always change, a bit like gossip—by the time you hear the story it has taken on more spice and flavour.

In this book there are many shared memories: coming home from school to a full biscuit tin or a kitchen of comforting aromas and the promise of a delicious meal that evening. What is a standout, however, is not only Mum's cooking—which was occasionally not great but all that mattered was that it was cooked by Mum—but the importance of the family dining together. Mealtimes mattered very much and it is this memory of family closeness that has remained vivid.

Cooking changes with the times: one family's meals changed when Elizabeth David's books became available in paperback, another's when a mother ventured on a health kick via Weight Watchers. The influence of celebrated author Charmaine Solomon—who demystified Asian cooking—is acknowledged, as is Margaret Fulton, who, through her column, guided readers with down-to-earth cooking tips. Ellen Sinclair, the long-time food editor of the *Women's Weekly*, likewise inspired generations of new cooks with her infallible recipes, introducing them to cuisines from around the world.

Generally our mothers had little time for fuss and whims and many worked outside the home. Ingredients were mostly *au naturel* supplemented with canned tomatoes, canned tuna and frozen peas. Interestingly, offal and seafood were not high on the list of favourite dishes. I distinctly remember cleaning raw tripe, to cook with onions in parsley sauce, and one of my all-time favourite childhood meals was lamb's fry cooked with bacon and tomatoes and served with fluffy mashed potatoes. In pensive moments I wish I could rewind the clock as I recall Dad fishing and bringing home chaff bags full of fresh crayfish, only for us to throw ourselves around groaning, 'Oh no, not crayfish again!'

Good dishes, like good manners, are never out of fashion—as the recipes in this book attest, good recipes outlast fads and trends. They are, put simply, too jolly good to be lost. Although constantly dazzled by futuristic food and giddy with technology, perhaps we should pause and reflect that there is nothing new in cooking, except what has been forgotten.

The pride and creativity of generations of mothers, who every day cooked meals for their families, paved the way for future cooks to follow and build on. This book is a salute to all of those who shared with their children the magic and luscious secrets of cooking—all with an abundance of patience and that most priceless of all ingredients, love.

‛ On gloomy winter days, when the early morning frost had taken to the air and maintained a lingering chill throughout the day, I would look forward to one of Mum's heart-warming casseroles. This was always eaten at the dining room table, with an open fire crackling in the background, and the family dog and cat cosily curled up by the hearth. ’

Ian Hemphill

‛ My mother, Elsa, lived for her family. Apart from the care she offered individually to each child, Mum's real love was expressed through her delicious food. ’

Damien Pignolet

'My mother shaped my interest in food by both her adventurous (for the times) cooking and by dragging me in my short pants school uniform to some very flash restaurants (again, for the times). I thank her, from the bottom of my stomach.

John Newton

'There was always room for another, and another, at our table. Should unexpected guests drop by, Mum could always conjure up something. All ages sat together, something continued with their beloved grandchildren.

Lyndey Milan

Robyn Archer and her mother, Mary Smith

My mother, Mary Louisa Smith (nee Wohling), is a proud and meticulous home-maker. A tailoress by profession, she was not an experienced cook when she married, but became a splendid provider. The late Clifford Charles Percival Smith was ever appreciative of the fine and full meals she served him for 55 years.

My childhood asthma made me a fussy eater as it felt just too hard to swallow, and my only-child status added to the privilege—I had few chores. I was spoiled in this sense. Mum didn't teach me to cook. The kitchen, like the housework, was her domain, and though I'm sure she offered, I guess I showed no interest; I had other fish to fry. I was a tomboy—no dolls, no domestics. Dad did the barbecues on his vast brick and funnel number out the back. Apart from special lunches at Coles Cafeteria or Balfours (past purveyors of the ultimate pastie) I had not been to a restaurant by the time I went to university.

Mary's Meatballs

Mum is now 85 years young. She lives in her own home, drives her car, and plays tennis every Tuesday, weather permitting. When I come home to stay a few nights with her, there are always freshly cooked meatballs in the fridge, along with lots of fresh vegetables, stewed apples and fruit in the bowl. She squeezes fresh orange juice for us every morning. Her meatballs are so much better than anything you can buy, and I never fail to indulge.

500 g minced beef or lamb
1 cup fresh breadcrumbs
1 egg
1 onion, finely chopped
¼ cup fruit chutney

1 clove garlic, crushed
salt and pepper, to taste
¼ tsp nutmeg
plain flour, for tossing
oil for frying

Combine the minced beef or lamb, breadcrumbs, egg, onion, chutney, garlic and seasonings into balls or small patties, toss in flour, fry until golden. Drain well.

We usually have them hot next to seasonal vegetables, but they're good in many contexts—party food on a platter, with a salad, amongst tapas (and you can vary them with different fancy chutneys), or make smaller balls and then combine with a tomato-based sauce and pasta.

Makes about 30 small meatballs or 8 large ones

My Footy Season Pea Soup and Crumpets

Pea soup and crumpets is a meal which seems to have originated through our small family's passion for Australian Rules football. I was born into a family of North Adelaide supporters: up the mighty Roosters! We went to the footy at Prospect Oval from the time I was around eight years old. There is simply nothing to beat returning home from the winter chill of an afternoon in the outer, to a hearty bowl of hot pea soup and crumpets on the side. To this day, if Mary and I go to a match (it's now more often the mighty Adelaide Crows), or even if we watch it on TV together, pea soup and crumpets are de rigueur as the conclusion to a perfect day.

onion, finely sliced lengthwise (ie, not into rings)
whatever raw vegetable is in the fridge—celery, carrots—chopped
dried mixed herbs—fling 'em in as you like
fresh parsley, chopped

small amount of oil
dried split green peas (I usually use about ⅔ of a 500 g packet, say 350 g)
bacon bones or smoked ham hock
boiling water
salt and pepper, to taste

In a big cookpot, sauté the onions and other chopped vegetables and herbs in a little oil. When the onion is soft but not yet golden, add the split peas and stir with a wooden spoon so they are touched by the oil. Fling in the bones or hock and add enough boiling water to cover the mixed bones (or ham hock) and vegetables by 6–8 cm.

Bring to the boil then turn back the heat and simmer with the lid on. Check regularly and stir. As the peas swell and soften, you may need to add more water depending on how thick you like your soup. Add salt and pepper to taste.

It always tastes better if you leave it overnight to cool then reheat, but if you can't wait (this meal often happens on impulse and requires an urgent dash to the shops to find ham hock), just wait till it thickens then toast crumpets and spread with whatever your heart allows.

Serves 6–8

Learning to cook

My first attempt at "cooking" while still at home was as a student at Adelaide University—and it was packet Rice a Riso. It was Diana Louisa Manson who taught me to cook. I was 27 and we devoured Elizabeth David; it was pre the Asian influence and cream was all the go. I have learned to cook now, never with cream, and it has become the infallible indicator that suddenly I have a few hours in which to take the foot off the frantic work pedal, shop for fresh ingredients, and cook at leisure. It is almost always spontaneous, hence my deep appreciation of late-opening shops.

Anil Ashokan and his mother, Leela Ashokan

The recipe here for Chemmeen Vevichatu is how my mother originally made this delicacy. It is a classic preparation of a typical home-style dish from Kerala, where my mother hailed from. At home this used to be a special occasion dish and was prepared in a terracotta pot that delivers a unique flavour. Because my mother was a vegetarian all her life, she wouldn't even taste this dish when she made it. She got us children to taste it before serving it. The leftovers (if any) would be stored in the terracotta pot and tasted even better the following day.

As I grew older and was training to be a chef, I would tell her not to cook the prawns as long as she used to (she would generally overcook them—just to make sure they were done) and would get a good laugh out of it when she would ask me to do that in my own kitchen!

Chemmeen Vevichatu

Prawns with Green Mango and Banana

Once she moved to Australia, my mother didn't have a stone grinder to make the spice mix, so she altered the ingredients. Instead of the dried red chillies, she used a teaspoon of red chilli powder and blended it in a food processor with a small red tomato, the grated coconut and the chopped ginger and turmeric. To add body and improve the consistency, she added a tablespoon of coconut powder at the end. Why the tomato? Mum found the green mangoes in Australia were less sour than the ones she was used to. It also adds colour to the sauce.

5 dried red chillies
warm water
1 cup freshly grated coconut
2.5-cm piece of ginger, peeled
　and chopped
½ tsp turmeric
½ green mango

1 small green banana
2 brown shallots
¼ cup salad oil
1 sprig curry leaves
600 g green prawns, shelled and
　de-veined
salt, to taste

To make the spice mix, break up the chillies, remove the seeds and soak in warm water to soften. Save the water for use in the sauce. Grind together the chillies, grated coconut, ginger and turmeric on a stone grinder or in a blender till a fine paste is obtained.

Peel the mango and banana and cut them into 1.5-cm cubes. Finely dice the shallots.

Heat a tablespoon of the oil in a terracotta pot or a heavy-based pan and drop in the curry leaves. Add the spice mix and the water from soaking the chilli. Bring to a gentle boil and simmer for a few minutes. Then add the prawns, mango and the banana. Season with salt. Simmer for a few minutes till all the ingredients are cooked, stirring gently.

Take the pan off the heat and keep covered. Separately, in a shallow pan, heat the rest of the oil and add the finely chopped shallots. Sauté till golden brown and pour the whole mix over the prawn and mango mix. Cover the pan immediately and set aside for the flavours to blend in. Serve with steamed rice.

Serves 4

Elayada
Steamed Rice Flour Dumplings in Banana Leaf

ೲಠಿ

Rice flour dough with a fresh coconut filling is steamed to make a simple tea time snack or a light dessert after a heavy meal. It's a very simple preparation, yet a little technical in getting the dough right for the best result. You can buy jaggery in stores that stock Indian foods, or use palm sugar, which is in most Asian supermarkets.

1 cup fine rice flour
pinch salt
boiling water
2 pods green cardamom

½ cup grated jaggery
1 cup freshly grated coconut
4 pieces banana leaf
   (approximately 20 cm square)

To prepare the dough, place the rice flour in a heavy-based pan and heat it on a slow, low heat to dry roast it so that it just roasts but doesn't colour at all. The flour needs to be stirred continuously to prevent it from sticking and burning. When the flour is well roasted, remove it from the heat and add a pinch of salt. Now add just enough boiling hot water to form a soft, yet firm, dough. Cover and set aside.

To prepare the filling, peel and crush the cardamom in a mortar. Place the grated jaggery in a heavy-based pan. Melt it over a moderate heat, stirring occasionally. Remove from the heat and add the powdered cardamom and the grated coconut and mix well.

To assemble the dumplings, divide the dough into four equal parts and form into balls. Place one ball in the centre of a banana leaf, press it down with palm of your hand and then shape into a circle evenly with your fingers. Wet your hand to prevent sticking. Spread the filling evenly over one half of the dough, then fold the leaf over to form a semi-circle. Repeat the process with the other balls of dough.

Place the dumplings in a steamer and cook for approximately 10 minutes. Serve warm or at room temperature.

Serves 4

Teatime

I remember my mother would make elayada for a snack
sometimes after we returned from school and would get it ready
for us in no time! Now that I have written this out in a recipe form
here, it seems a lot more complex that it actually is. Just four
ingredients and some hot water is all it takes to make this delicacy
and it is light in kilojoules too. Happy memories!

Maggie Beer and her mother, Doreen Pearl Ackerman

My mother was quite amazing. Amazing in her joy for life even through times of such hardship where many would have crumbled. She was a really good cook, having been mentored by my dad who was obsessed with good produce, even back in the 1950s. He was way ahead of his time and Mum took it all on with her natural gusto.

Mum and Dad worked very hard when I was at high school, so I would prepare all the vegetables for the evening meal and they were, as in most families, the 'meat and three veg' during the week. But no matter how simple, everything was the best cut—the crumbed veal chops from bobby veal, the best cut of rump, the pig's head to make the brawn in summer, the roast chook on Sunday that had been dispatched in the backyard, freshest fish always cooked with the head on, and oysters you opened yourself.

Simple though the food was most times, any celebrations like birthdays and Christmas were veritable feasts—something that continues in my family now.

Macaroni Cheese

My mother often made this rich and luscious dish when we had relatives coming to dinner. Now when I think about the small oven she had to work with, it makes sense that she chose to bake a dish that took maximum advantage of the limited space available. Mum never wrote down a recipe in her life, so I only have the memory of what she did to go by. I remember that, even when I was a child, she'd use the sharpest possible cheese she could find (in those days it was a New Zealand Epicure cheese). I have contributed my own touch, adding roasted pumpkin and Persian feta.

1¼ kg Japanese or Queensland blue pumpkin, peeled, seeded and cut into small chunks
4 stalks rosemary, leaves picked and chopped
sea salt
extra virgin olive oil, for cooking
¼ cup verjuice
2 litres milk
2 fresh bay leaves

160 g unsalted butter, chopped
160 g plain flour
1 tbsp freshly grated or ground nutmeg
250 g parmigiano reggiano, grated
400 g large macaroni
150 g Persian goat's feta, crumbled
250 g cheddar, grated

Preheat fan-forced oven to 200°C. If you have a standard oven, preheat to 220°C.

Line a baking tray with baking paper, then add the pumpkin and rosemary, season generously with salt and drizzle with olive oil. Roast for 30 minutes or until pumpkin is tender and starting to brown. Take the tray out of oven and drizzle the verjuice over pumpkin. Return the tray to the oven and continue cooking until verjuice has evaporated.

Meanwhile, heat the milk with the bay leaves in a saucepan over high heat until almost boiling, then remove it from the heat and leave it to infuse for 10 minutes. Remove and discard the bay leaves and keep the milk hot.

Melt the butter in a saucepan over medium heat until nut-brown. Add the flour and cook until the flour and butter come together, stirring for several minutes. Remove from the heat and slowly pour in the hot milk, using a whisk to incorporate and prevent any lumps from forming. Return to the heat and stir with a wooden spoon for another 10 minutes or until the sauce is shiny and coats the back of the spoon. Add the nutmeg and grated parmigiano reggiano, stirring continuously until the cheese has melted. Taste the sauce to see if any salt is necessary; take care to only season with salt after you've added the parmigiano reggiano as it can be salty enough. Cover the surface of the sauce closely with plastic film to stop a skin from forming and set aside until needed.

Cook the macaroni in a large saucepan of boiling salted water until al dente, then drain and place in a large mixing bowl. Add the cheese sauce to the macaroni and mix through well, then add the pumpkin and toss through gently. Gently stir in the crumbled feta. Transfer the macaroni mixture to a large 10-cup baking dish (mine is a 40 × 30 × 5 cm), top with grated cheddar and bake for 10–20 minutes or until brown. Serve immediately.

It definitely needs to be served with a bitter leaf salad alongside; my stock-in-trade one is made with radicchio, rocket and witlof, dressed with a good vinaigrette.

Serves 12–16

Golden Syrup Dumplings

Sweets weren't a common occurrence in our family. There were a few tried and true like bread and butter pudding and baked rice custard very occasionally, but only once in all my childhood did Mum make these dumplings. I was probably about 4 years old and we were living in Rose Bay. Around 1949, blackouts were the normal thing. I remember one blackout with Mum lighting a candle in the kitchen as we sat and ate these dumplings with the storm raging outside. It's probably my first real food memory of taste, place, safety and comfort all combined.

1 cup self-raising flour
pinch salt
1 tbsp butter

1 egg, whisked
50 ml milk
runny cream, to serve

SAUCE
1½ cups golden syrup
½ cup water

60 g butter

To make the dumplings, sift the self-raising flour with a pinch of salt into a bowl. Rub in the butter then add the whisked egg and stir to combine. Add the milk slowly till the dough resembles a scone mix. Set aside and make the sauce.

Combine all sauce ingredients in a large frypan with a fitted lid. Bring to the boil to amalgamate and turn down to a simmer.

Meanwhile, cover a dish with a large piece of baking paper. Flour your hands and roll the dough into balls the size of 20-cent pieces, putting all the dough balls on the paper as you make them. Slip the balls off the baking paper all together into the syrup. Cover the pan with the lid and cook for about 10 minutes, then turn the dumplings over to cook on the other side for another 10 minutes.

Remove the dumplings with a slotted spoon and serve with the sauce and a jug of runny cream.

Serves 4–6

Shopping

I didn't ever learn to cook from either Mum or Dad but I did learn to shop with Mum to choose what was best and freshest and so learnt from such an early age the importance of that. Cooking was truly so natural to me I didn't realise how much I had learnt by osmosis in my childhood.

Allan Campion and his mother, Theresa Campion

Earliest memories of my mother's cooking revolve around hearty and wholesome Irish food of the 1960s like winter broth cooked with pork sausage or corned beef and cabbage. Oxtail soup with home-made soda bread was another staple. Not fancy, but perfect for a growing family in Dublin. Sunday drives regularly led to picking wild blackberries which were transformed into the most amazing jam. Theresa's apple tarts were legendary.

Emigration to Australia in 1973 brought with it unfamiliar ingredients. A Greek neighbour taught my mother how to prepare eggplants for moussaka. A wok made its way into the kitchen and a brick barbecue was built in the backyard. My mother's recipe repertoire expanded at a great rate with dishes such as rolled beef olives, steak and onions and even the occasional rabbit curry if Uncle Eddie had a successful weekend shooting.

My siblings and I were always welcome to help in the kitchen and interested in what was for dinner. I have no doubt this contributed to my becoming a chef and food author.

Oxtail Soup

Oxtail soup is delicious and rich—perfect for a warming meal. It's a soup that requires a hefty 3–4 hours of simmering to draw out the best flavours.

1 kg oxtail, cut into 3–4 cm pieces
plain flour for dusting, seasoned with salt and pepper
olive oil, for cooking
2 onions, diced
2 carrots, diced
3 celery stalks, diced
2 leeks, sliced

¼ cup tomato paste
3 cups red wine
6 cups beef stock
2–3 bay leaves
2–3 sprigs of thyme
salt and freshly ground black pepper
chopped parsley

Coat each piece of oxtail with seasoned flour, shaking well to remove any excess flour.

Heat a large saucepan over a medium heat and add a generous splash of oil. Add the vegetables and cook for 5–10 minutes, stirring regularly. Remove the vegetables from pan and set aside.

Return the pan to a medium–high heat, add more oil if needed and cook each piece of oxtail until browned on all sides. Add the tomato paste and cook briefly for 1–2 minutes, stirring occasionally.

Return the vegetables to the pan and add the red wine, stock, bay leaves, thyme, a pinch of salt and the pepper, and bring to the boil. Remove any scum as it rises to the surface and reduce the heat to low. Allow the soup to simmer for 3–4 hours.

Remove the oxtail pieces and set aside to cool. Puree the soup and strain the liquid into a clean saucepan.

When oxtail pieces are cool enough to handle, remove all meat from the bones and dice finely. When ready to serve bring the soup to the boil, add the oxtail meat, let it return to the boil and check seasoning. Add chopped parsley.

Serves 6

Soda Bread

This old-fashioned Irish recipe uses baking soda and baking powder for rising and the dough is simply stirred together, shaped and baked until golden. It's excellent served warm with butter and jam.

2½ cups wholemeal self-raising flour
2½ cups self-raising flour
2 tsp baking powder
1 tsp bi-carb soda

1 tsp salt
2 cups buttermilk, or milk soured with lemon juice
additional buttermilk, for brushing

Preheat the oven to 210°C. Line a baking tray with baking paper.

Sift together the flours, baking powder, bi-carb soda and salt. Stir in the buttermilk and mix until combined to a firm dough.

Shape the dough into a round, about 4 cm high, on the lined baking tray. Slash a deep cross into the top of the bread, then brush it with additional buttermilk.

Bake in the preheated oven for 20 minutes. Remove from oven and brush with buttermilk. Reduce oven to 180°C and return the bread to the oven and cook for a further 40 minutes. A perfectly cooked loaf will sound hollow when tapped on the bottom. Wrap in a dry tea towel as it cools—this will help keep moisture in.

Serves 6–8

Rhubarb Crumble

Stewed rhubarb with custard or rice pudding were both favourite family desserts. This is my version of a fruit crumble my mother regularly made when I was a teenager. It's a great thing for teens to make themselves as it's simple and delicious.

2 bunches of rhubarb
¼ cup caster sugar
2 tbsp water

150 g soft butter, diced
250 g plain flour
¾ cup soft brown sugar

Trim off the leaves and root ends from the rhubarb and discard and cut the stems into 2-cm chunks.

Heat a heavy-based pot over medium heat. Add the rhubarb, caster sugar and water. Reduce the heat to low, cover with a lid and cook for 5–10 minutes, stirring often. The rhubarb should be reduced to a chunky paste. Remove from the heat and allow to cool.

Preheat the oven to 180°C.

Rub together the soft butter, flour and brown sugar until they resemble fine breadcrumbs.

Place the stewed rhubarb in a baking dish, top with crumble mixture and bake in the preheated oven for 20 minutes, or until golden brown. Serve with cream or custard.

Serves 4–6

Cheong Liew and his mother, Cheong Sow Keng

I grew up in Kuala Lumpur. We were the local poultry wholesalers selling live chicks, chickens and chicken feed. Our 'shop house' was near a junction of three roads and we lived upstairs—as is the way in shop houses even today. At that time life was fairly traditional for our family and my grandmother wielded matriarchal power. She was the head chef and organiser of the family. Most of our food was from my grandmother's province. She did not cook Malay or *Nonya* dishes. My mother was allowed to help but not to cook. After Grandma died, we had to make our own sweets for Chinese New Year and for the first time my mother was in charge of making the celebration tapioca pudding and rice flour biscuits, rather than being a mere helper.

My memories of that time are mainly of my grandmother's birthday and her funeral, my cousin's wedding and the many hours I sat in the kitchen preparing sour dough buns, cleaning shark fins, removing the young shoots from the lotus seeds, cutting wood, stoking the kitchen fire and cleaning vegetables. Other strong memories are of making chilli sauce, and grinding rice to make flour using two flat granite stones the size of car tyres as a rotating mill. In retrospect, this was all part of my apprenticeship.

When I was about 14, my father decided to move about 8 km away to a farm near a Malay *kampong* (village) and the shop became our Cantonese restaurant, where I worked during school holidays. It was a time of loosening traditions and absorbing other influences and becoming a 'modern Chinese family' in our own eyes. Before my grandmother's death we had not cooked many curry dishes; after her death this changed. We started introducing other styles partly because we liked the flavours and partly because we simply did not have the knowledge and time for traditional cookery which my grandmother had possessed.

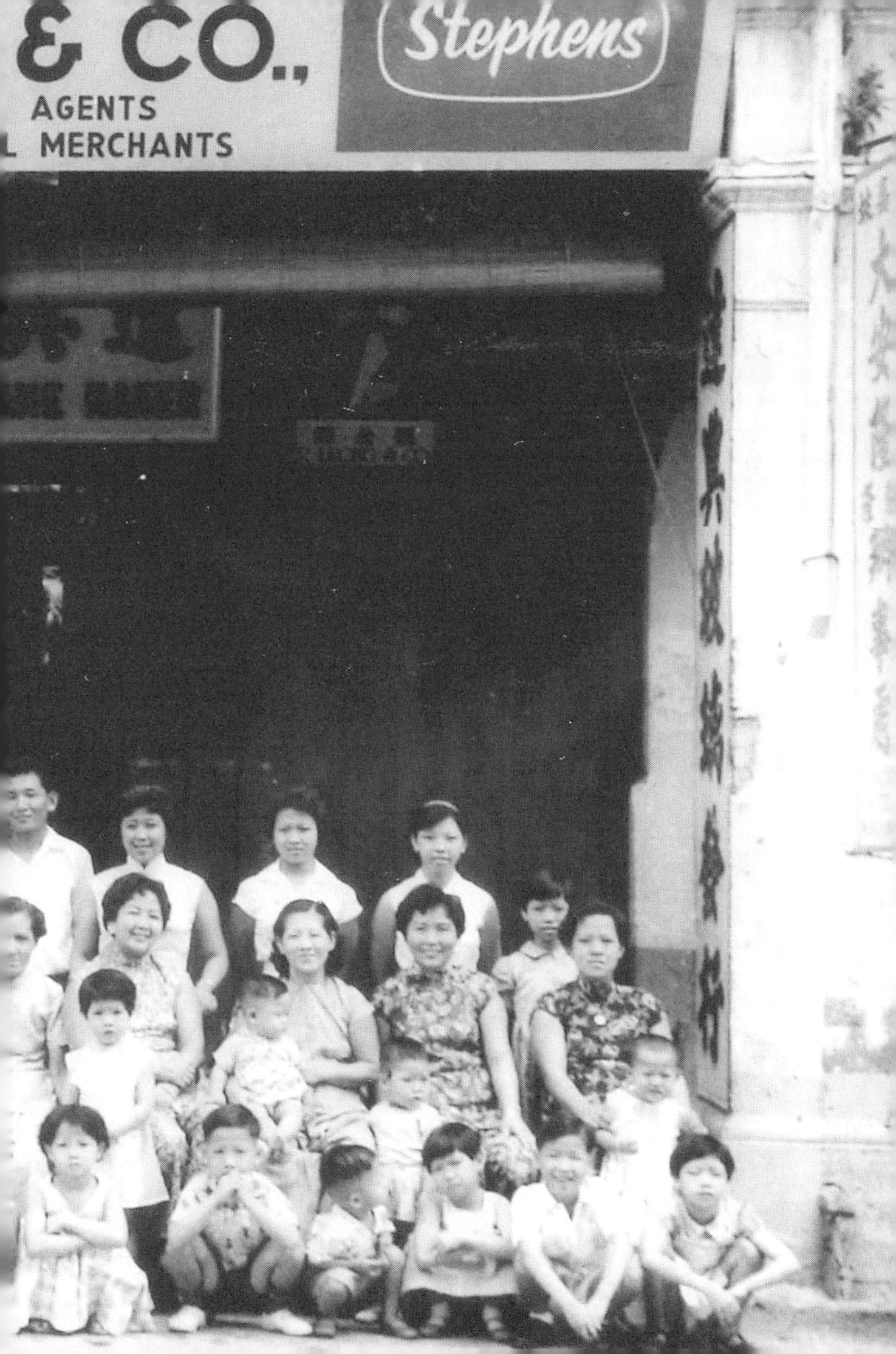

& CO.,
AGENTS
L MERCHANTS
Stephens

Grandma's Fun Kwor

Every Chinese village traditionally has its particular style of fun kwor *depending on ingredients. I remember Grandma making this style for her own birthday. She always had a brigade of several daughters and daughters-in-law as well as cousins, friends and neighbours to help out when the big preparation day came around. Fun* kwor *are the easiest dim sum (the dumplings served for Chinese yum cha) recipe of the lot.*

Fun kwor *are either shallow-fried in oil or steamed—my grandmother preferred them steamed. The women would sit in a circle and make the* fun kwor, *and the kids would also have a go with the scrap dough but the aunties had the nimble fingers necessary for perfect packaging. It was wonderful to watch. Now both the women and the men of the family make them.*

FILLING
1 tbsp corn flour
1 tbsp water
1 tbsp olive oil
80 g dried shrimp, roughly
  chopped
80 g pork fat, finely minced
240 g pork fillet, finely minced
160 g Chinese salted turnip,
  finely chopped

160 g water chestnuts, diced
1 bunch garlic chives, finely
  chopped
40 g roasted peanuts, roughly
  chopped
1 chilli, finely minced
1 tbsp rice wine
½ tbsp salt
1 tbsp sugar

PASTRY
pinch salt
375 g wheat starch
80 g tapioca starch

400 ml boiling water
1 tbsp lard, melted

To make the filling, mix the corn flour and water in a small bowl. In a large frypan, heat the oil and sauté the dried shrimp, then add the pork fat, pork fillet, Chinese salted turnip, water chestnuts, garlic chives and peanuts and fry until the mixture is fairly dry but glazed. Add the chilli, rice wine, salt and sugar and thicken with the corn flour mixture. The filling should be slightly on the sweet side.

To make the pastry, add the salt to the wheat starch and tapioca starch in a medium-sized bowl. Stir the boiling water into the starch to form a dough. Turn onto a floured surface and knead until the dough's colour and texture are even and it comes to a shine, taking care not to knead too much. Incorporate the lard into the dough and knead a little longer.

Roll the pastry to 3 cm thick by 20 cm long and divide into cubes. Roll each cube into a ball and flatten and roll out the pastry into a circle with a 6-cm diameter. Place the filling mixture in the centre and seal the edges by folding over like a 'pastie'. Pinch the edges together until they equal the original thickness of the pastry.

Steam the dumplings in a Chinese steamer or large covered plate over boiling water for 10 minutes and serve piping hot on a large plate.

Makes 20–25 dumplings

Steamed Atlantic Salmon Fillet with Spring Onions and Coriander

Wonderfully delicate, slightly oily, and always available fresh, this fish lends itself to the Chinese approach and is economical because the slices are quite thick and a couple of pieces are enough for a family of six. How can a couple of pieces suffice? Because this will be one dish among several—served as part of a meal in which rice is the staple. The idea is not to have fish with rice but to have rice with fish. This is an important aspect of Chinese etiquette.

1 kg Atlantic salmon, skin left on, rib bones removed
salt
freshly ground black pepper
2 tsp rice wine
6 spring onions, finely shredded, white and green separated
2-cm knob ginger, finely shredded
3 tbsp white chicken stock
1 tbsp light soy sauce
1 tsp sugar
3 tbsp peanut oil
fresh coriander

Season the salmon with salt, pepper and half the rice wine. Place it in a Chinese steamer and steam over a gentle heat for about 3 minutes— the meat should still be pink. Strain off the juices. Place the fish on a serving dish, then cover it with the shredded spring onion (white only; reserve the green) and ginger.

Bring the stock to the boil in a small saucepan, remove from the heat and add the soy sauce, remaining rice wine and sugar and pour this over the salmon. Heat the oil in a pan until smoking and add the green of the spring onion then pour over the fish.

Garnish the serving plate with fresh coriander and serve immediately.

Serves 6 as part of a meal

Cooking for others

When we lived on the farm, I remember digging up tapioca roots.
My sister Kwei-lan would make this into a pudding and whatever
was left we would sell to the villagers for pocket money. We were
expert at killing, dressing and roasting chickens on an open fire,
and we collected eggs for cooking omelettes or "purse" eggs.
This was the time I started to cook for others. I would fry sweet
potato leaves as a vegetable dish with dried shrimp and chilli,
cook omelettes with baked beans—an early experience in being
creative with tins—and deep fry chicken as my mother had
taught me.

Vic Cherikoff and his mother, Lucy Cherikoff

The pic is a favourite one of me and my mum, Lucy, shortly after I was born in 1955. It was taken on a Sydney beach, just coming into summer. I grew up in Lindfield but we moved around a lot to different Sydney suburbs and to Adelaide for a few years. My parents worked in my grandfather's bakery/factory which made meringues and American-style cookies, just as they had in Hong Kong from the 1930s to 1950s. Cherikoff Cake Shop was still in Nathan Road (Hong Kong) until just a few years ago. My family ownership of the brand stopped when they left China in 1952, fearing the imminent arrival of the Communist Chinese. My father's family had walked out of Russia and into China a generation before and the risk of Communist uprising meant staying was not an option. Luckily the British arranged for expatriation of many White Russians and my family had a choice: San Francisco, Auckland or Sydney. A one-in-three chance and I might have been born elsewhere and never helped launch a wild food industry.

My food education was quite different from that of my mates. While they brought Vegemite, Devon, cheese or peanut butter sandwiches for lunch to school, I might have had leftovers with either a European or Chinese slant. I remember my mother's aunt coming over for regular four-day weekends, starting on a Thursday. My mum and aunt would go shopping in Chinatown in Sydney's Dixon St and bring back swags of what my friends would call 'weird food'. This included 100-year-old duck eggs, chicken feet, barbecue duck, sauces, unrecognisable dried foods, spices and flavourings, wonton skins and other exotica. What followed was a three-day feast—breakfast, lunch and dinner with Szechuan, Mandarin and Cantonese dishes, soups for breakfast, multi-course meals and everything savoury. These meals would vie with those of a Chinese restaurant as my mum's aunt was a very large, extremely passionate, and very talented cook.

On other occasions, my mum had Russian friends over or her own mother would visit and the pilmenny, piroshky and pilmicchi were the fare of the day. Some were fried, others boiled. Then there were the blinchiki, kasha (buckwheat) and borscht. Great for a Siberian winter but probably a little out of place for summery Australian fare.

The upshot of my upbringing was not to go into food but to university where working in nutritional science I (eventually) discovered my life path—wild foods. I taught myself to cook as a prerequisite to teaching chefs about the new foods I had discovered and was commercialising. I have found and am currently working on an extract from an Australian plant which kills all sorts of cancer cells—so far ovarian and gastric cancer cells have successfully been killed in lab tests. I only wish I had had the chance to give this to my mum—she might still be with us.

Chicken Billy

I must admit to hating celery as a food, particularly raw. That and parsley are two foods I just don't like. However, this dish was the only way I'd eat the celery which ended up cooked really well and my mum would slice it quite finely. I still hate parsley.

I have no idea why the name caught on in our family but the dish could be cooked in a 'billy' on a campfire. However, my mum used her trusty electric frypan. Mum would always bake the whole chicken and section it Chinese style so the carcass ended up in 12 pieces. This was another dish served on steamed rice, a common carb in the Cherikoff household. We didn't eat much potato or pasta but there were always lots of vegetables.

I learned to cook rice by the absorption method, filling the saucepan with rice up to the first finger joint, adding water up to the second finger joint, bringing to the boil before putting on a lid and turning down the heat to a simmer—15 minutes and perfect rice every time. I hated eating sticky, tasteless, over-cooked boiled rice at my friends' places and remember trying to teach their Australian mums to cook rice 'properly' on several occasions. It didn't go down well and reminds me of showing chefs the intricacies of using wild herbs in more recent times and having them still revert to crucifying the aromatics by adding the herbs at the wrong time. Old habits do die hard.

1 medium onion, chopped	oil for frying
3 celery stalks, finely sliced	400 g can tomatoes
1 red capsicum, diced	1 baked chicken
250 g mushrooms, sliced	soy sauce, to taste

Stir-fry the onion, celery, capsicum and mushrooms until soft in a little oil and add the tomatoes (roughly chopped). Section the baked chicken and add to the vegetables. Season with soy sauce to taste and a little pepper. Heat through and serve on steamed rice.

Serves 4

Beef Stroganoff

This brought together the Asian trick of flouring meat to keep it juicy when cooking—using soy sauce as a seasoning to enhance juice retention (far better than salt)—and the generous use of sour cream in the decadent European tradition. The beans were also a real favourite of my mum. It became a running gag that whenever a vegetable was needed, out came the green beans. I do recall that a little honey and butter on them, and on fresh peas, made my young palate find them OK to eat.

500 g topside or rump, fully
   trimmed
plain flour
peanut oil for frying
butter

500 g sliced mushrooms
dash of Worcestershire sauce
dash of soy sauce
150 ml sour cream

Partially freeze the meat to make slicing easy then cut into fine strips about 3 mm thick, cutting across the grain of the meat. Dust with the plain flour to coat completely.

Heat a large pan to medium-high heat and add the peanut oil and butter to coat the bottom of the pan. Add the meat, spreading the slices out over the pan so as not to lose too much heat in any one spot. Stir-fry briefly and then add the mushroom slices. Continue cooking until the meat begins to brown.

Add a dash each of the Worcestershire and soy sauces and just a little water to help deglaze the pan. Add the sour cream and turn down the heat and simmer until the flavours combine.

Serve over steamed rice with steamed French runner beans and some raw red capsicum.

Serves 4

Ten Shilling Cake

The 10 Shilling Cake was a favourite birthday cake of mine from the age of around 12 and my mother religiously made one every year, up until my forties when sadly she died when misdiagnosed symptoms led to terminal pancreatic cancer. It's also called Eight Brothers Cake. My mum re-named it when she first started making it in the 1960s because the all-up cost was 10 shillings. This made it a very expensive cake at the time, so it was certainly a decadent dessert for us. Delicious freshly made, it just got better and better over the next few days as the barely baked pastry would soak up the custard. We'd stretch it out as long as we could, and my sister and I would fight over who got the biggest piece whenever the serves were being divvied up.

PASTRY
250 g butter
2 cups plain flour
1 cup self-raising flour
3 tbsp sour cream

2 tbsp sugar
2 eggs
½ vanilla bean, finely chopped

CUSTARD CREAM
1 litre milk
½ vanilla bean, finely chopped
¾ cup caster sugar
3 heaped tbsp corn flour

4 eggs, separated
1½ cups milk, extra
125 g unsalted butter

To make the pastry, rub the butter and flours to fine breadcrumb consistency. Add the sour cream, sugar, eggs and vanilla bean and knead well but handle minimally so as not to melt the butter. Roll the pastry into a log and cut into eight pieces. Refrigerate for 30 minutes while the custard is made.

To prepare the custard cream, bring the milk and vanilla to boil in a saucepan. Meanwhile blend the sugar, flour, egg yolks and remaining milk in a bowl. Add some of the boiling milk to this mixture, stirring continuously to prevent lumps forming. Then add to the remaining hot milk in the saucepan and cook while constantly stirring, until thickened. Remove from heat and add the butter, allowing it to melt into the custard. Beat the egg whites until stiff and fold into the custard.

Preheat the oven to 150°C. Heat an ungreased baking tray.

To assemble the cake, roll out a piece of pastry, leaving the rest in the refrigerator on hot days. The idea is not to attempt to roll it out to exactly cover the tray as there's not enough dough to do this and still handle the sheet you make. Just roll it out as much as possible, place it on the heated tray and spread it out, pushing the dough to the edges with your hands, making a really thin pastry sheet. It'll be almost see-through in some sections. Bake until pale brown, turning the pastry tray around (to ensure even cooking), unless using a fan-forced oven in which case it won't need turning. Repeat with the remaining seven pieces and assemble the cake as the pastry sheets are baked.

To do this, place the first pastry sheet on an appropriate board or platter. We had a specially cut piece of plywood which Mum would wrap with foil, although I'm not too sure of the sense of this these days as aluminium foil really shouldn't ever come in contact with food as plasticizers and aluminium metal are implicated in so many diseases (cancer, Alzheimer's etc). Use baking paper or parchment instead. Anyway, smother the pastry with custard, add another just-baked pastry sheet and repeat, finishing with a custard layer. Cut the edges all around to neaten the cake and place the cut sections onto the top of the cake so they all fall in the same direction. Finish with a dusting of fine sugar. Keeps refrigerated (covered with baking paper and foil) for up to a week and a half but there's no chance it'd last that long in our house.

Jill Dupleix and her mother, Rosemary Dupleix

I don't know how she did it. Mum used to cook for a family of six every day, plus all the school lunches, the cakes and biscuits that were so much a part of country living, and the feeding of seasonal workers such as shearers, and make it all seem effortless. Then she would entertain, doing crown roasts of lamb filled with peas, or chocolate éclairs, making the choux pastry and the ice-cream herself. So I always saw cooking as a source of pleasure rather than as a chore, and I loved 'helping out', which in hindsight, probably wasn't very helpful. Our eating was very much linked to the land— peas from the paddock, peaches and nectarines from the orchard. Milk came from the cow, eggs from the chooks, meat from our own sheep. She made her own butter, brewed her own beer and pickled her own onions. We all ate so well, and had absolutely no idea how lucky we were. (I do now! Thanks, Mum.)

Boiled Artichokes with Butter

My mum was an all-or-nothing cook—if asparagus was in season, we ate asparagus, if it was time for corn, we ate corn—and when the huge artichoke plant at the back of the meathouse was laden down with big, fat artichokes, boy, did we eat artichokes. Since then, I have never been one to stuff, puree, or fiddle about with artichokes in any way. I just do as Mum did: boil them until tender, and serve them steaming hot, with a huge block of butter in the middle of the table.

As you peel off each leaf, you scrape it along the butter, then scrape it again with your teeth, filling your mouth with buttery, creamy, earthy artichoke. The leaves get increasingly 'meaty' as you work your way in to the tender heart, and the discarded leaves pile up on your plate as if it were autumn. Definitely a recipe to share only with friends, family or lovers.

6 large or 12 medium artichokes   250 g block of fresh salted
1 lemon   butter

Choose artichokes that feel heavy and full, with leaves that are tight and large. Trim off all but 10 cm of the stem. Trim the tops of the artichoke leaves with scissors, and pull off a few of the hard outer leaves. Rub the cut surfaces with lemon to stop them going brown.

Cook the artichokes whole in a large non-reactive pot of boiling, salted water for 15 minutes or more, depending on the size. They are cooked when you can tug a leaf out of the base fairly easily. Drain upside down for a few minutes, then turn right way up and serve warm with butter. Important: the butter must be as fresh as a daisy, without that awful orange, sour-tasting border of old butter, and should not be melted.

Serves 4

Old-Fashioned Egg and Bacon Pie

When Mum started making a big egg and bacon pie, we knew we were in for a treat—either a picnic in the bush, or a day spent water-skiing at the local lake (Bullen Merri in Victoria). The kids would all scatter and do their own thing as soon as we got there, but we somehow magically knew when Mum started cutting up the egg and bacon pie on the tail-gate at the back of the station wagon.

4 sheets frozen puff pastry,
   thawed
4 streaky bacon rashers, rindless
10 free-range eggs
100 ml milk

3 tbsp flat-leaf parsley, chopped
sea salt and freshly ground black
   pepper
grated nutmeg
1 extra egg, beaten

Preheat the oven to 190°C. Line a lightly buttered 22- or 23-cm pie dish with half the pastry, patching to fit as necessary, and allowing it to overlap the edges.

Chop the bacon and fry in a dry frypan until lightly cooked. Set aside to cool.

Whisk 6 eggs with the milk, parsley, sea salt, pepper and nutmeg.

Arrange half the bacon on the pastry, and pour in the egg mixture. One by one, crack the remaining eggs into a cup and gently slip into the mixture. Top with the remaining bacon.

Brush the pastry rim with the extra beaten egg and lay the remaining pastry over the top. Crimp the edges with the tines of a fork, and trim off excess pastry.

Brush the top with beaten egg and bake for 15 minutes, then reduce the heat to 170°C for a further 25–30 minutes or until golden brown.

Leave in the dish to cool for 30 minutes before removing. Allow to cool to room temperature before slicing.

Serves 6–8

Granny's Goo

My grandmother, Dolly May Campbell, used to make this pud, then my mother Rosemary made it, and now I make it, but Mum and I, and my brother and my sisters, still call it Granny's Goo. I'm sure everyone knows it already because it's a very trad old Australian pud, but for me, it's very linked with wood-burning stoves, scarred old wooden spoons and recipe books written in perfect copperplate. I love it because it works every time, making its own gooey chocolate sauce as if by magic, and because it makes the whole kitchen smell like my grandmother's.

125 g self-raising flour
2 tbsp cocoa powder
pinch salt
100 g soft butter

100 g caster sugar
4 eggs, lightly beaten
½ tsp pure vanilla extract
3 tbsp milk

SAUCE
125 g soft brown sugar
2 tbsp cocoa powder

250 ml boiling water

Preheat the oven to 180°C.

Sift together the flour, cocoa and salt.

Cream the butter and sugar until pale. Beat in the eggs, one at a time, and the vanilla. Fold in the flour mixture and the milk alternately, mixing well. Spoon the mixture into a buttered ovenproof 18-cm baking dish, or into four individual 1-cup moulds.

To make the sauce, pour the boiling water over the cocoa and brown sugar in a heatproof bowl and stir until dissolved.

Pour the sauce over the pudding, and bake for 40–50 minutes (20–25 for individual puddings), or until the top has formed a crust, the centre is cooked, and bottom is runny. Serve with custard, cream, ice-cream or thick yoghurt.

Serves 4

Lucio Galletto and his mother, Bruna Martini

I come from a little village by the sea on the Italian Riviera, and we used to eat a lot of seafood. Mostly it was economical seafood like octopus, mussels and anchovies, all delicious of course.

I remember as a child going to the dock, when Dantin, the local fisherman, came back with his boat. My mother and I would wait while his wife, Angió, would beat the octopus over the rocks to tenderise them and then she would call out to my mother to go and get them!

Braised Baby Octopus

Moscardini in Umido

There was never a written recipe, but I remember the ingredients. I make this octopus recipe every now and again at home with my family and it takes me back in time.

150 ml extra virgin olive oil
2 cloves garlic, finely chopped
1 kg baby octopus, cleaned and
   cut in half
120 ml white wine

6 ripe tomatoes, peeled, seeded
   and diced
salt and pepper
1 cup chopped parsley

Heat the oil in a heavy-based pan on low heat and cook the garlic for about a minute or until it starts to change colour.

Add the baby octopus and sauté for 10 minutes, mixing often with a wooden spoon. Pour in the white wine and let it evaporate, still on a low heat, for about 3 minutes. Then add the tomatoes, season with the salt and pepper and cook for another 35 minutes on medium heat, stirring regularly.

Sprinkle on the chopped parsley. Mix and serve immediately with some crusty Italian bread.

Serves 4 as an entrée

Fish with Olives and Herbs
Pesce con Olive e Erbe

On special occasions my mother would purchase a whole orata (similar to our bream) from Angió and cook it in a very Ligurian style with olives, potatoes, pine nuts and mixed herbs. Buonissimo! What a celebration.

butter
100 ml extra virgin olive oil
20 bay leaves
a whole snapper or bream
   (about 2 kg), filleted into
   2 fillets
500 g potatoes, peeled and
   sliced thinly
salt and pepper
1 tbsp fresh finely chopped
   rosemary leaves

1 tbsp fresh finely chopped
   oregano leaves
1 tbsp fresh finely chopped
   thyme leaves
1 cup white wine
100 g black olives (Ligurian)
1 tbsp pine nuts
1 tbsp fresh breadcrumbs

Preheat the oven to 220°C.

Take a baking dish (large enough to fit the two fish fillets in a single layer) and rub it with butter. Brush 3 tablespoons of olive oil over the bottom of the dish. Place the bay leaves on top of the oil, then put the 2 fillets of fish on the bay leaves and arrange the sliced potatoes around them. Season with salt and pepper, splash over 2 more tablespoons of olive oil and bake in the pre-heated oven for 10 minutes.

Mix together the rosemary, oregano and thyme leaves.

Take the dish out of the oven and pour the white wine over the fish and potatoes. Sprinkle over the black olives first, then the mixed herbs, then the pine nuts and finally the breadcrumbs. Put it back in the oven for another 10–12 minutes to complete the cooking. Serve hot.

Serves 4

Sun-dried Tomatoes

Pomodori Essicati al Sole

Sure you can buy sun-dried tomatoes, but my mother never did! She used to pick ripe tomatoes from our vegetable garden when they were at their best at the end of July and the beginning of August and then dry them herself. She would serve them with a favourite of ours, bollito misto (mixed boiled meats), but nowadays they are mostly served as part of an antipasto. I will not give quantities because it is up to you how much you want to make. All you need are:

sunny days
ripe tomatoes
sea salt

extra virgin olive oil
basil (optional)
chilli (optional)

Wash the tomatoes and pat dry. Cut them in half and remove the core, and using a teaspoon remove the seeds and any excess water. Place the tomatoes on large trays and sprinkle generously with sea salt. You must now let the tomatoes rest in sunshine for three or four days, bringing them inside at sundown. When you can see that the top side is dried, you turn them over, sprinkle lightly with salt again and give another three or four days of sunshine.

When dried they can be place in a glass jar and covered with oil, ready for use. You can add basil or chilli at this stage if you like.

Gabriel Gaté and his mother, Pascaline Gaté

My mother has always shared with me her love of good food. She is *très gourmande*! I grew up in the Loire Valley and my parents grew most of the vegetables, herbs and fruits that we needed. We also had a tiny vineyard and made our own wine.

Both my mum and grandmother prepared the family meals, and from an early age encouraged us kids to contribute by asking us to do small jobs like peeling vegetables or making a salad dressing or mayonnaise. As I got older, I became more skilful and confident and this is certainly the reason I became a chef.

Some of my most memorable moments in the kitchen were helping to garnish the delicious home-made fruit tarts with raspberries, strawberries or apple.

Now 86 (at the time of writing), my mother still lives in the village where I grew up, and when I visit her each year at the end of spring we go to markets together and enjoy special meals at restaurants.

Rabbit, Carrot and Prune Casserole

Rabbit was one of our favourite meats and during the winter months wild rabbits were sometimes brought to us by relatives. We also kept our own rabbits which we ate during the cold months of the year.

1 rabbit, 800 g–1.2 kg
1 tbsp olive oil
1 tbsp chopped thyme
1 small brown onion, chopped
1½ tbsp plain flour
about 12 pitted prunes
1 cup red wine

2 medium carrots, peeled and cut into 2-cm thick slices
1 cup veal or chicken stock
salt and freshly ground black pepper
4 tbsp chopped parsley
1 clove garlic, finely chopped

Cut the rabbit into seven pieces (the four legs, and the body, cut in three).

Heat the oil on high heat, then brown the rabbit pieces on all sides. Add the thyme and stir well for 10 seconds. Add the onion and cook for 2 minutes. Sprinkle in the flour and stir well. Add the prunes and wine and bring to the boil. Add the carrots and stock and season with salt and pepper.

Cover with foil and a lid and cook gently for 2 hours or until the rabbit is tender and the flesh falls easily away from the bone. Stir in the parsley and garlic just before serving.

Serves 4

Egg and Celeriac Salad

When I was a boy, grated celeriac was as popular as grated carrots, and during the season my mother prepared this first course several times a week. I still love it.

1 egg yolk
1 tsp hot mustard
1 tsp red wine vinegar
salt and freshly ground black
  pepper
3 tbsp vegetable oil, e.g. peanut,
  canola

about 500 g celeriac
2 tomatoes, diced (optional)
the heart of a butter lettuce,
  about 8 leaves
2 hard-boiled eggs
2 tbsp finely chopped chives or
  parsley

In a large bowl place the egg yolk, mustard, vinegar and a little salt and pepper and whisk until very smooth. Slowly pour in the oil, whisking continuously to make a thick sauce.

Peel and grate the celeriac. Add the celeriac to the sauce with the diced tomatoes and stir well.

Arrange the washed lettuce leaves on plates and top with the celeriac salad.

Peel and chop the hard-boiled eggs. Scatter the eggs over the top of the salad, sprinkle with chives or parsley and serve.

Serves 4

Crepes with Raspberries and Cream

French pancakes are thin and are made using plain flour. At home in France, our family made them regularly as a dessert. My mother would mix the batter, then every member of the family would cook and flip their own pancakes. It was so much fun.

1 cup plain flour, sifted
1 egg
about 1 cup milk
1 tsp cooking oil
1 tbsp butter

about 500 g raspberry jam (or other jam)
about ¼ cup rich cream
about 200 g raspberries, or fruit of your choice

Place the flour in a mixing bowl. Make a hollow in the centre and pour the egg and half of the milk into the hollow. Using a whisk, first mix the eggs and milk together, then gradually incorporate the flour, slowly adding the rest of the milk to form a smooth, thin mixture.

Strain the batter through a fine strainer and refrigerate for at least 20 minutes or until required. If you are in a great rush, you can use it immediately but the pancakes will not be as smooth.

Heat the oil and butter in a crepe pan, or small frying pan, until it turns a light golden colour, then whisk this melted butter and oil mixture into the pancake batter.

Return the pan to high heat and when hot, pour in enough pancake batter to cover the bottom of the pan. Twirl the pan in a smooth motion to form a thin, even pancake. When the upper half of the pancake starts to become dry and the lower half is golden brown, pick it up with a spatula and turn it quickly onto the other side. After browning the second side, remove the pancake and place it on a plate.

Without adding any more butter or oil to the pan, make the rest of the pancakes in the same way. If a pancake begins to stick, wipe the pan with absorbent paper, melt a little butter in the pan and make the next one.

Spread each pancake with a little raspberry jam and cream. Top with a few fresh raspberries, fold the pancakes and serve.

Makes 6–8 pancakes

Ian (Herbie) Hemphill and his mother, Rosemary Hemphill

Herbs and spices have always been a part of my life. My parents, John and Rosemary Hemphill, owned a citrus orchard that metamorphosed into a plant nursery and ultimately became a herb and spice business. They pioneered Australia's love of herbs and spices in the 1950s, and Mum was the first Australian to have a book published about herbs (*Fragrance and Flavour*) in 1959. Since that title, she and my father went on to write several more books on herbs and spices which were published in Australia and overseas.

During this time my mother was always experimenting with new recipes that used herbs and spices. It seems as though every evening was peppered with a new taste sensation, and I firmly believe that during this privileged childhood, I subliminally absorbed, as if by osmosis, an appreciation of food and the transformations that can be achieved with the judicious use of herbs and spices.

Fennel Seed Sausage

One of my favourites was Mum's Fennel Seed Sausage, and these days I find it quite amusing that the latest trendy Italian sausage that everyone 'must try' is a fennel seed one. This is actually a large sausage that is generally eaten cold and sliced and is great on sandwiches and with salads. This recipe is from Fragrance and Flavour with a few measurement changes to acknowledge the move to metrication!

2 eggs
1 kg beef mince
4 cups soft breadcrumbs
2 tbsp whole fennel seeds
1 onion, chopped

2 tsp salt, more or less to taste
1 tsp coarsely ground black
   pepper
½ cup dry breadcrumbs

Beat the eggs. Put the meat, soft breadcrumbs, fennel seeds, chopped onion and salt and pepper in a bowl and mix well together.

Have a clean floured cloth ready. Form the mixture into a sausage on the cloth, and roll the cloth round it well, tying each end with cotton string. Put the sausage into a large saucepan of boiling water, and cook for 2½ hours. Lift out carefully onto a plate, unfold the cloth and slip it away from the sausage. Roll the sausage in the dry breadcrumbs and leave to cool.

Casserole of Beef

In the 1950s we had no central heating in our weatherboard cottage in Dural. On gloomy winter days, when the early morning frost had taken to the air and maintained a lingering chill throughout the day, I would look forward to one of Mum's heart-warming casseroles. This was always eaten at the dining room table, with an open fire crackling in the background, and the family dog and cat cosily curled up by the hearth.

2 kg roast beef (chuck steak would work)
1 cup olive oil
250 g bacon, cut into fairly big pieces
2 cloves garlic, peeled
2 peeled tomatoes

12 black olives, pitted
2 tsp dried rosemary leaves
1 glass red wine
2 tsp salt (more or less to taste)
2 tsp freshly ground black pepper

Preheat the oven to 120°C.

Cut the beef into thick rounds. Heat the oil in a casserole on top of the stove, put in the meat and seal on both sides. Lower the heat and add the bacon, garlic and tomatoes. Simmer a little longer (about 15 minutes) and add the olives, rosemary, red wine, salt and pepper. Put the lid on the dish and cook in a slow oven for 2 hours.

Spiced Tea Cake

From time to time Mum would have friends around for morning or afternoon tea. Coming home from school, my even-then keen sense of smell would alert me to the culinary morsels Mum had been making. After a reasonable amount of begging and whining on my part, she'd always save something for me and Dad to have when the party was over! Having always loved cinnamon (and I mean the true Cinnamon zeylanicum, not the stronger cassia), this Spiced Tea Cake was, and still is, one of my favourites.

30 g butter at room temperature
½ cup caster sugar
1 egg
1 cup self-raising flour
¾ cup milk

1 apple, peeled, cored and thinly sliced
2 tsp mixed spice
15–20 g butter, extra
1 tbsp cinnamon for topping

Preheat oven to 160°C. Smear a 21-cm cake tin with butter and then a dusting of flour to prevent the cake from sticking.

Cream the butter and sugar. Add the egg and beat well. Gently fold in the sifted flour and milk alternately.

Lay the sliced apple in the bottom of the cake tin and sprinkle with mixed spice. Pour over the batter and bake in a moderate oven until cooked—about half an hour.

Carefully loosen the cake from the sides of the tin, and turn out onto a plate or wire cooler. Immediately place small dots of butter over the apple base of the cake (now the top) and sprinkle with ground cinnamon. Return it to oven until butter has melted, then repeat process. (Yes, the tea cake went back in the oven on the wire rack as it is only in long enough to melt the butter. My grandmother used to put more butter and spice on it up to three times!) This is best served while still warm from the oven, but is also delicious when cold.

Pocket money

᷾ᤛᤛᤛ

' I would earn my pocket money picking herbs on the family farm,
Somerset Nursery, that later became Somerset Cottage. Numerous
school holidays and weekends were spent helping Dad propagate
cuttings, and picking lavender, lemon verbena, rose petals and
scented geraniums for the pot pourri that my father would make.
I remember many a season when our home was strewn with
bunches of drying herbs. '

Alex Herbert and her mother, Gillian Herbert

When I wasn't growing up in my mother's kitchen, I was growing up in my grandmother's and my aunt's kitchens. Food was constantly being planned and prepared around family gatherings and celebrations.

Food is infectious—wherever we went, so did good food. Annually we traipsed to the ski lodge where everyone would cook and share their meals. My mother still has the big black stock pot that she would take. Whatever was in it would just tick away quietly while we careered down the slopes developing even greater than usual appetites.

Chocolate éclairs, custards, meringues and sponge cakes were standard grub at home, the recipes having been passed down through the women in the family.

Once I had progressed from just sitting on the bench watching Mum cook, I used to prepare the ingredients, laying them out in little dishes and then cooking them up, pretending that I was Bernard King giving a cooking demonstration.

Beef Stifado

Just as my mother has been my influence, she admits that there have been other women in her life. Elizabeth David's much-used books have always lined my mother's cookbook shelves. David's recipes for Beef Stifado and Apricotina have long become family staples. In fact her Beef Stifado recipe forms the basis of my Beef Cheek Pie at Bird Cow Fish.

1½ kg beef cheeks
freshly ground black pepper
sea salt
150 ml red wine
1 bay leaf
5 sprigs of fresh thyme
2 allspice berries

5 black peppercorns
olive oil and butter, for browning
2 large brown onions, finely
   chopped
50 ml balsamic vinegar
chicken stock, to cover
freshly chopped flat-leaf parsley

Trim the beef cheeks but leave whole and season generously with black pepper and sea salt. Marinate the meat overnight in the wine, bay leaf, thyme, allspice and peppercorns.

The following day, drain the cheeks from the liquid, reserving the marinating liquid for later use. Take a pan of sufficient size to contain all the ingredients and, in a little oil and butter, lightly brown the cheeks on all sides then set aside.

In the same pan brown the diced onion, deglaze with the reserved marinating juices and the balsamic vinegar and return the cheeks to the pan. Cover with chicken stock, seal the pot and gently braise at 130°C until the cheeks fall apart when encouraged with a fork—2–3 hours.

Allow to cool in the fridge overnight. Remove the cheeks from their jelly and reduce this liquid before returning the cheeks to heat through. When ready to serve, adjust the seasoning and add a little red wine vinegar to taste with generous amounts of freshly chopped flat-leaf parsley.

Serves 6–8

Lemon Delicious

My mother and I cooked a lot together from the wonderfully worn pages of Margaret Fulton. Lamingtons, Rock Cakes, Chocolate Puddings, Fried Rice—you name it, the list goes on. But this recipe for Lemon Delicious is the one that springs to mind first. I still cook this recipe and even serve it in my restaurant. Set the prepared moulds out in a baking dish lined with a cloth—this will be your bain marie.

75 g unsalted butter, cubed
1 tbsp finely grated lemon rind
　from washed lemons
375 g caster sugar
4 eggs, separated
450 ml full cream milk

⅓ cup plain flour
¼ tsp baking powder
½ cup freshly squeezed lemon
　juice, pips removed but not
　strained
pinch of cream of tartar

Preheat the oven to 200°C. Lightly grease 8 small individual ovenproof ramekins or 1 large dish.

Cream the butter, lemon rind and sugar together in a food processor. Add the egg yolks and mix well.

Gradually add the milk, alternating with the flour and baking powder sifted together, beating between each addition. Scrape down the sides from time to time to ensure the mixture is smooth. Finally with the motor still running add the lemon juice in a slow stream. Transfer this custard base mixture to a large bowl and set aside.

Place the egg whites in a spotlessly clean, dry bowl and whisk, add a pinch of cream of tartar and continue whisking to semi-firm peaks.

Fold a small amount of the egg white, about ⅓, into the custard base with a metal spoon (a whisk is even better) and gently combine well. Then fold this mixture (again gently) back into the remaining egg whites.

Divide the mixture evenly among the prepared ramekins in the bain marie. Place the bain marie in the oven and fill with warm water to halfway up the side of the ramekins. Bake uncovered for approximately 35 minutes. The puddings should be lightly coloured and spongy to touch.

Dust with icing sugar and serve with fresh cream.

Serves 8

Iain Hewitson and his mother, Sybil Hewitson

We were a very close family and we ate well. I suppose ours was an old-fashioned family. Mum was the matriarch. She was the one who just kept the whole thing going. You look back and you think to yourself, 'Gee, mothers were pretty tough in those days'.

We used to have to help when my mother made and bottled her famous home-made tomato sauce—so I think that's probably the first dish I ever had anything to do with. A family favourite was a fish and chip butty (with my father's famous crispy beer batter, of course) topped with mother's tomato sauce. The sauce was pretty good with cheese fingers too.

One of my mother's all-time favourites was her version of the ubiquitous tuna casserole—a dish she spent many hours slaving over. First she would make a classic mornay sauce with plenty of top quality cheese and thick country cream. Then a fresh tomato sauce of which any Italian mama would be proud, into which she would fold butter-sautéed sliced onion, fresh herbs and chunks of canned tuna. Of course, herein lay the problem—canned tuna. And, while I love my mother dearly, this was not one of her greatest culinary creations, because the canned stuff overshadowed everything, including the lovingly made sauces. Because of this it was many, many years before I could bring myself to eat fresh tuna. Eventually, with much prodding, I plucked up enough courage, tasted the real thing, and discovered one of the culinary delights of the world. (Interestingly, in recent years I have revisited my childhood and decided that I now actually like canned tuna mornay—admittedly with a few additions, such as fresh corn.)

When I was a kid, one of my favourite treats was soldiers on toast with Vegemite (crusts cut off and cut lengthways into three or four pieces), which I then dipped into my soft-boiled egg. Wonderful stuff! I also remember the family's mushroom foraging expeditions—nothing fancy, just big juicy field mushrooms which my mother simply cut in four and sautéed in lots of butter with chopped parsley and a good squeeze of lemon juice.

My father was a school principal in Levin (New Zealand) and a wonderful gardener. When we had Sunday lunch together—roast leg of lamb, of course, and pavlova too—us kids had to help Dad harvest the vegetables from the garden. I am sure this has something to do with why I like to whip up vegie dishes with a reasonably major role in the meal today.

We didn't have a lot of money, but there was always a decent proportion of our family budget spent on food. They were pretty happy times.

Chicken Pie with a Potato Crust

My mother often served this on a bed of rice, rather than with mash.

6 large potatoes, peeled and cubed
1 tbsp vegetable oil
1 tbsp butter
1 large onion, sliced
10 button mushrooms, sliced
2 rindless bacon rashers, sliced

10 chicken thigh fillets, cubed
freshly ground salt and pepper
3 tbsp plain flour
2–3 cups chicken stock
2 tbsp cream
1 tbsp chopped fresh parsley
a little hot milk

Preheat the oven to 220°C.

Cook the potatoes in lightly salted boiling water until tender and then drain.

While the potatoes are cooking, heat the oil and butter in a heavy-based pot and gently sauté the onion, mushrooms and bacon for about 5 minutes. Add the chicken and seasoning, and cook until the chicken changes colour. Add the flour, turn down heat and cook for a few minutes. Add the stock, cream and parsley, and gently simmer until thick, stirring regularly.

While the chicken is cooking, mash the spuds with a little hot milk. Then season.

Put the chicken mixture in an ovenproof serving dish, top with mash and cook in the oven for about 20 minutes.

Serves 6

Devilled Lamb's Kidneys on Toast

I was pretty pleased to score an invitation to dine at my mate Charlie's. Not only did the sun shine and the wine flow freely, but a surprise was in hand with a delicious course of an almost forgotten delicacy—lamb kidneys. I was instantly reminded of palmier days when rarely a week went by without at least one plate of awful offal gracing the Hewitson table. Those were the days, when everything from tripe to tongue to liver was regarded as a special treat, and when mums prided themselves on their ability to transform these cheap cuts into tasty meals. Tip: kidneys, to be tender, should be cooked no more than medium—so pink in the centre please.

10–12 lamb kidneys	¼ cup chicken stock
vegetable oil	1 tbsp Dijon mustard
½ medium-sized onion, finely chopped	a splash of Worcestershire sauce
6 button mushrooms, sliced	freshly ground pepper and salt
1 garlic clove, crushed	Tabasco sauce
⅓ cup cream	4 slices country-style bread
	2 tbsp chopped fresh parsley

Remove the membrane from the kidneys, cut in half lengthways and, with a sharp knife or kitchen scissors, cut out all the sinew. Then cut each half into 4 even pieces. Heat the oil in a large pan and brown the kidneys on all sides, in three or four lots. Remove and set aside.

Wipe out the pan, heat a little more oil and gently sauté the onion, mushrooms and garlic until soft. Mix the cream, stock, mustard, Worcestershire and ground pepper well into the mixture and reduce over a high heat until thickened.

Add the salt and Tabasco to taste, then return the kidneys to the pan and simmer, very gently, for about 3 minutes.

Grill or toast the bread, place on individual plates, spoon the kidneys over and sprinkle with chopped parsley.

Serves 4

Home-made Tomato Sauce

This is my mother's famous tomato sauce, which you obviously make in a larger quantity than given here, purely and simply because it is delicious with almost anything.

1 kg ripe tomatoes, cored and chopped
250 g Granny Smith apples, peeled, cored and diced
150 g onions, chopped
150 ml white wine vinegar

200 g sugar
1 tsp allspice
1 tsp ground cloves
1 heaped tsp sambal oelek (or any other chilli paste)
1 tsp table salt

Put all the ingredients in a large pot, mix well and bring to the boil. Simmer for about 1¼ hours, regularly stirring. Then blend and cool (if keeping, pour into sterilised jars).

Pavlova

This began life as my Auntie Peggy's recipe. My mother then added her variations and, more recently, we added a few of our own.

icing sugar
6 egg whites
500 g caster sugar
½ tbsp corn flour
½ tbsp white vinegar

½ tbsp vanilla essence
whipped cream
passionfruit pulp
sliced fresh fruit, e.g.
 strawberries and kiwifruit

Preheat the oven to 140°C–150°C. Line a baking tray with paper and dust with icing sugar.

Beat the egg whites in a very clean, dry bowl for 5–6 minutes until stiff peaks form. Then, while continually beating, add a tablespoon of caster sugar at a time until fully incorporated.

Combine the corn flour, vinegar and vanilla, and slowly pour into the meringue mixture, whisking until stiff peaks re-form.

Then place the meringue mixture in the centre of the baking tray and shape with a plastic spatula, making sure the edges are straight. Cook in the oven for 40–50 minutes until crispish on the outside and some cracks appear on the surface. Allow to cool.

Generously spread with cream and garnish with the passionfruit pulp and fruit.

Serves 8–10

Peter Kuruvita and his mother, Liselotte Katherina Kuruvita

My mum, in my eyes as well as the eyes of many others whose lives she has touched, is a saint—one of the warmest and most generous and giving human beings, who always makes time for her friends and family. All her grandkids adore her and can't wait to see her. She is tenacious, too, and will get things she has set her mind on done at any cost, as long as it does not hurt anyone.

Times were not always easy for our family. I was born in London, and we moved to Colombo, my Dad's home town, in 1967. In 1974 Dad packed us all up suddenly and moved us to Australia—it was a pretty bad time in Sri Lanka and we had friends here.

Over the years and despite whatever difficulties there were, Mum always supported her three sons in anything they wanted to do. She taught me how to be self-sufficient from a young age, much to my protests—I could sew, cook, clean and was gifted with a social conscience long before I left school. The recipes here are our Austrian favourites directly from her.

Stuffed Capsicums with Tomato Sauce

∾⊙⊙∾

I love Mum's little notations in this recipe.

10 green capsicums
1 onion, chopped
1 clove garlic, crushed
300 g minced meat, half beef,
   half pork
salt

pepper
2 slices of bread, soaked in
   water
parsley, chopped
1 egg

Make an incision around the top of the capsicums and remove the 'lids', clean out the seeds and the white pith. The cookbook says 'pour boiling water over them and leave them for 20 minutes'. I simply immerse them for a minute in a pan of boiling salted water, then lift them out using the handle of a cooking spoon and set them aside to drain. Meanwhile, make the tomato sauce. (See recipe below.)

To make the stuffing, fry the chopped onions, then add the garlic. (The cookbook does not mention garlic, but because it's such a healer I like to add it.) Add the minced meat (the cookbook says 'minced leftover roasted or boiled meat') and pan fry until the meat has a nice colour. Add salt and pepper, the squeezed out bread (the cookbook says 100 g boiled rice) and last of all the chopped parsley. Add an egg to bind, then spoon the mixture into the prepared capsicums. Replace the lids and stand them upright into a large pan with the tomato sauce. Gently simmer them in a covered pan for an hour.

TOMATO SAUCE

1–2 onions, chopped
olive oil, for frying
½ tsp sugar
pinch salt

1 tbsp plain flour
1 cup water
500 g tomatoes, cut into quarters

Fry the onions in a little oil. When they are golden, add the sugar and salt, plus the flour sprinkled over to make a thickened base for the sauce. Add the water and tomatoes (I also add ketchup!) and simmer for a few minutes while making the stuffing, stirring occasionally.

Vanilla Crescents
Vanille Kipferln

಄ᢀᜤᏑ

Here's what Mum said when I asked for the recipe: 'I am going to send you Mirli's recipe, the one I always made is with ground almonds, but hers, with ground hazelnuts is much tastier.'

280 g plain flour
210 g butter
70 g sugar
100 g ground hazelnuts

1 egg
pinch salt
vanilla sugar plus icing sugar,
    to coat

Sift the flour into a bowl. Add the butter and sugar, and use your fingertips to rub in the butter until the mixture resembles breadcrumbs. Add the hazelnuts, egg and salt. Knead to make a dough, then form into a roll. Wrap in plastic wrap and put into the fridge until needed, especially in summer, otherwise the pastry is not easy to work with.

Preheat the oven to 180°C. Grease a baking tray.

Divide the roll into portions to roll out to make the individual crescents. Using your hands, roll each portion out into a 2-cm thick roll—like a thick piece of rope. Cut crosswise into 5-cm lengths and shape each length into a little crescent shape.

Place them on a baking tray and bake until they are golden—about 10 minutes. Allow them to cool for a minute while you combine the vanilla sugar and icing sugar in a bowl.

Place the warm crescents carefully in the bowl of sugar to coat. Place spaced out on a wire rack to cool. Store in a container with a tight-fitting lid. Sometimes they keep longer if the container is kept in the fridge.

Mum's Austrian favourites

Wiener schnitzel is a favourite, but with lean pork flattened with a cleaver, then covered with flour, beaten egg and breadcrumbs (in that order). Fry them in a generous amount of oil (we used lard) so that they become crispy and puff up. Another favourite is potato salad (*Erdäpfel Salat*). Boil kipfler potatoes, peel, cut into slices, pour over olive oil and cool. Pour over a dressing made with apple cider vinegar, water and sugar together with finely chopped onions and a little hot English mustard. If you like (and we did, until we became worried about weight) add some mayonnaise (home-made in the olden days, now I buy it). Top the salad with chopped fennel, if you want, or finely chopped spring onions.

Carolyn Lockhart and her mother, Phyllis Kershaw

My mother inherited her father's love of gardens and it was almost a condition of their marriage that my father become a keen gardener too. My parents had great faith in manure, and as children my brother and I were sent into the street with dustpan and broom to collect the droppings of any passing horse. There was a red-painted watering can on the back porch where the men of the house were supposed to pee. When diluted and mellowed the liquid became 'very good for the azaleas'. They were certainly magnificent.

When we moved to the country Mum and Dad were in heaven. With manure, compost, love and hard work, they soon had magnificent vegetable and flower gardens.

Mum had a keen interest in healthy eating and our meat came with lots of delicious vegetable dishes and salads. When a new blender came into our lives everything turned green from copious amounts of 'life-giving' parsley. She once attempted green milkshakes but my brother and I rebelled.

Vegetable Slice

This simple dish works well either hot or cold. It is good on its own or to accompany grilled meat. It can be made ahead and is very useful if you have vegetarian friends over for a barbecue. The base vegetables of carrot, cabbage and onion can be added to with any leftover vegetables and extra herbs. Pieces of leftover cheese, including blue, can be included. The top can be embellished with slices of tomato, capsicum rings or chopped bacon.

2 large onions, finely chopped
olive oil
3 eggs
2 cups finely sliced cabbage
1½ cups grated carrot
½ cup chopped parsley

any other chopped fresh herbs such as thyme, oregano and basil
2 cups grated tasty cheese
½ cup grated parmesan (or more to taste) or chopped bacon
freshly ground black pepper

Preheat the oven to 160°C. Grease or spray with olive oil an 18 × 27-cm pan with sides about 2 cm deep or a small baking dish.

Wilt the chopped onion in a pan in a little olive oil until soft. Lightly whisk the eggs and mix the onions and all the remaining ingredients together in a bowl.

Spoon the mixture into the greased pan or baking dish and pat down firmly. Top with a little more parmesan or chopped bacon if desired. Cook for about 1 hour or until the slice is set and top is golden and bubbling.

Serves 4, or 6 as side dish

Fresh Lemon Refrigerator Cake

This was a rich and pretty party cake that I remember my mother and aunts liked to serve at engagement parties, kitchen teas etc. It had to be made a day ahead, which was convenient. They also invented a pineapple version, and a chocolate one which was very like tiramisu. You need a ready-made sponge cake for this recipe—a packet cake (two layers, unfilled) a couple of days old is best.

3 rounded tsp corn flour
½ cup caster sugar
3 eggs, separated
1 cup milk
1 tbsp butter
juice and grated rind of 1 big
   lemon

1 bought or made-up packet
   sponge cake
2 tbsp Cointreau, optional
300 ml cream
1 small lemon, for decoration

Place the corn flour, sugar and egg yolks in top of a double boiler. Mix thoroughly, add the milk and butter and bring water slowly to the boil, stirring mixture all the time with a wooden spoon.

Cook until thick and smooth. Remove from the heat, add the lemon juice and rind. Mix well. While still warm (not hot), fold in the stiffly beaten egg whites.

With a sharp knife, cut the sponge cake into thin layers (do not worry if they break a bit).

Butter a 20-cm spring-form pan and line the bottom and sides with a thin layer of cake. Cover the bottom with a generous layer of the lemon mixture, then a layer of sponge cake, repeat, finishing with a layer of the sponge cake. Cover with plastic wrap and refrigerate overnight.

Two hours before serving whip the cream stiffly. Carefully remove the sides of the spring-form pan, leaving the cake on the metal base. Place on a serving plate (a piece of damp paper napkin will stop it from sliding).

Cover the top and sides of the cake with whipped cream in rough swirls and decorate with very thin slices of lemon and coarsely grated rind. In summer my mother would decorate the base with frangipani blossoms for a gala effect.

Christmas Shortbread

My mother was very proud of her shortbread. She said including ground rice was the secret. The shortbread was always cut in small rectangles and decorated with rows of holes made by a fork (I was allowed to do this part). This recipe is exactly as she wrote it. All I have done is convert Mum's measures to metric. And of course you need to roll out the pastry before cutting it. In Mum's day, instructions were very brief.

280 g butter
140 g caster sugar
340 g plain flour

110 g ground rice
1 tsp salt

Preheat the oven to 150°C.

Cream the butter and sugar. Work in the dry ingredients. Knead dough for a couple of minutes on a marble slab.

Roll the dough out to ½ cm thick and cut into rectangles 3 cm by 5 cm. Place on flat oven trays. Prick rows of holes with a table fork. Bake in slow oven (150°C) until golden, about 30 minutes in a fan-forced oven, and 45 minutes in a standard oven.

Makes 60

The garden

My grandfather lived in a rambling house surrounded by a magic garden just round the corner from our own home in Longueville. It was the family house where my mother and her three sisters had been born. I can remember, from the age of about two, following "Grangy" around the garden picking flowers for a tiny posy, tasting fresh peas or the first strawberries and learning the names of plants. When he dug in the garden beds we always seemed to unearth bits of old china dolls or little broken tea sets along with the wiggly worms.

A huge palm tree full of birds sat in the middle of the lawn, deep red blackboy roses climbed the fence, sweet peas could be picked in huge bunches and there were rows of vegetables and herbs with climbable fruit trees and even a cool, mysterious "bush house" of wooden slats where he grew lily of the valley, a favourite of my grandmother who had died many years before. Mum later said (in her nineties) that she had lived such a long and healthy life because of all the garden-fresh, organic fruit and vegetables she ate as a child.

Kate McGhie and her mother, Susannah Chambers-McGhie

I feel very lucky born a farmer's daughter into seven generations of a family who worked and respected the land. Our farm, in Victoria's western district, produced everything we ate—there were Berkshire and large white pigs, dairy cattle who provided us with milk, clotted cream, cheese and whey for the piggery, sheep, goats and beef cattle. Our veggie garden was huge (it took about 100 steps in one direction and 200 in another), and the potato patch was two acres with five different varieties. The orchard was shared: the lower third for possums, the top third for birds and we had the middle section—everyone was happy.

My mum innately understood the symbiotic relationship between the land, her beloved garden and the kitchen which extended to family around the table.

She made absolutely everything from scratch including pastry of every kind—puff, short crust, suet, rough puff and hot water pastry. Flour and sugar were the only staples bought, and the only tinned food was sardines, which were, and to this day still are, my secret treat.

Cheese was made, meat pickled and smoked, bread baked and a pantry as large as a small home beautifully preserved the bounty of the land. There were big muslin balls dripping the clear nectar of overly ripe tomatoes, ginger beer, preserves, conserves and eggs rubbed with grease and layered in straw, fruit wine, salted vegetables, herbs drying, meats curing. It was a marvellous culinary Aladdin's cave.

Mum, like other country cooks, was innovative in the kitchen because every day she had to put a meal on the table based on what was in season or in the pantry. She had to be extra creative when cabbages were in season. Added to this she catered for the farm hands and harvesters who required meals in the paddock around the clock.

Christmas was always a special celebration as up to 18 people would come and stay for a few days and the excitement of preparing the food was the highlight of the year—fattening the poultry, pickling the pork for her boiled cushion bacon, and of course making the puddings (the joy of family stirring, coins added and wishes made), mince pies and festive treats.

My mum had a big and generous heart and spirit which was reflected and tasted in her cooking. She represented family and love. However to this day I have never found her recipe for 'leftovers' which appeared weekly, usually following the Sunday roast.

Our farm was on 'God's gourmet trail', the homesteads known by the local vicar or priest to have a 'good table'. They somehow managed to coincide their visits with noon (a large three-course hot meal) or afternoon tea when 'the full monty' of baked cakes, biscuits and sandwiches were served on doilies on tiered dishes. My mum would have had a 3-hat rating for her 'table'.

It was an idyllic life which immersed me in a life-long affair with food.

Corned Beef with Cloves

Just the mere mention of this homely dish has friends beating a path to my door. We had our own meat and when breaking down the carcass the white roast, as it was then called (now known as girello or eye round, the better end of the silverside, lighter in colour because it is from a less used muscle) was pickled in a brine with molasses (sometimes honey or brown sugar), allspice and bay leaves.

about 2 kg piece pickled girello
1 large onion, peeled
whole cloves
2 bay leaves
1 tsp whole black peppercorns
1 tsp grated nutmeg or a piece
   of blade mace

1 tbsp brown vinegar
1 tbsp soft brown sugar
vegetables, to taste (carrot,
   parsnip, onion, potato,
   cabbage)

SAUCE
butter
plain flour

parsley, finely chopped
mustard

Rinse the meat in cold water, place in a large heavy-based pan and cover with cold water. Bring slowly to the boil and then immediately drain the water off.

Cover the meat again with fresh cold water, and add the onion generously studded with cloves, bay leaves, peppercorns, nutmeg, vinegar and sugar. Bring this slowly to the boil, removing any froth that rises to the surface. Reduce the heat, cover and gently simmer, allowing about 1¼ hours per kg of meat or until it appears to be starting to shred. The gentle simmering will allow the characteristic flavour to emerge and will also tenderise the beef.

Vegetables seem a natural addition when cooking corned beef. Chunks of carrot and parsnip, whole peeled onions and potatoes can all be added about halfway through cooking time. Continue the slow simmer until the vegetables are cooked and the meat can be easily pierced with a fork. Wedges of cabbages can be added in the last 5–8 minutes. You can also add about 2 cups of apple cider to the stock, halfway through cooking time, to intensify the flavour. To serve, lift the meat and vegetables from the pan, cover and keep warm.

To make a sauce, blend an equal quantity of butter and plain flour together in a pan and stir over a medium heat for 1 minute. Add ladles of hot meat broth, stirring continuously until you have a thin sauce. Add finely chopped parsley and mustard to taste. Slice the meat and serve with the sauce spooned over, accompanied by the vegetables.

Serves 6 with ample leftovers

Slumpy Berry Pie

Mum's pie used berries as the base for a simple, loose scone dough that 'slumped' over the berries creating a dish that was crisp on top and soft underneath. Whatever berries were at hand were used—blackberries, mulberries or gooseberries were favourites—they are so juicy with a tart wine flavour. It was always served with scalded cream.

5 cups fresh berries
1 cup sugar
1 cup plain flour
1½ tsp baking powder

¼ tsp sea salt
¾ cup milk, or cream, soured
  with 1 tsp lemon juice
2 tbsp butter, melted

Preheat the oven to 180°C.

Put the berries into an ungreased 5–6-cup pie dish and sprinkle over ¾ cup of the sugar.

Sift the flour, baking powder and salt into a bowl. Add the remaining sugar with the soured milk and butter and whisk until smooth, then pour over the berries. Don't worry if the berries are not completely covered as they will be seen bobbing through the topping when cooked. Bake for 40–45 minutes or until top is golden.

Serves 6

Mum's Chocolate Fluff Sponge

There were no electric mixers so all beating was done by hand—a tiresome job with the occasional rewards of licking the bowl. When sponges were a bit floppy and uneven, Mum would say imperfections tasted better. And they did. The cake rack was covered in a clean tea towel to prevent wire marks on the top of the sponge. For fetes and special afternoon teas, Mum showed me how to decorate sponges by placing a paper doily or a stencil on top of the sponge, dredging it with sifted icing sugar and then carefully removing the doily to reveal a decorative pattern.

For light fluffy sponges, fresh eggs at room temperature are an essential ingredient. To ensure good volume use a large metal spoon with a cutting and sweeping action when mixing in the flour. Any grease in the bowl—even a speck, or yolk with the egg whites, will prevent the sponge from rising.

4 free-range eggs, separated
¾ cup caster sugar
2 tsp golden syrup
1 tbsp plain flour
½ tsp bicarbonate soda

1 tsp cream of tartar
½ cup corn flour
2 tsp cocoa powder
1 tsp ground cinnamon

Preheat the oven to 180°C. Grease two 20-cm round cake pans with butter and lightly dust them with caster sugar.

Beat the eggs whites to soft fluffy clouds and gradually add the sugar, beating until the mixture is glossy. Add the yolks one at a time and mix well after each addition. Fold in the golden syrup using a large metal spoon.

Sift the dry ingredients together and fold into the egg mixture. Divide the mixture evenly between the pans and bake for 20 minutes. To test when cooked, lightly touch the sponge in the centre—it should spring back. Turn the sponges out onto a wire rack and allow to cool. When cool, sandwich together with whipped sweetened cream flavoured with vanilla essence and dust with icing sugar.

Baking day

My mum was a no-fuss cook who did not worry about failures or shortcomings of her kitchen or equipment. She taught me that cooking was magic, transforming an ingredient into something completely different. Every Saturday Mum and Nana had a baking day and the aromas of the kitchen of those days are forever etched in my food memory. As a tot I was plonked on the massive kitchen table where I watched the alchemy, as two country women wove their magic with ingredients picked only minutes before.

Making choux pastry, Mum broke every rule there was: she'd leave it on the stove, duck outside to pull a few weeds, hang out the washing or feed a couple of orphan lambs, then came back to the stove, give the mixture a few quick stirs and onto the tray. The result was large, crisp clouds of pastry, later filled with clotted cream and dusted with icing sugar. On special occasions the pastry was made into dainty swans and elegantly displayed on a silver stand.

Joanna McMillan Price and her mother, Isobel McMillan

My mum was a domestic science teacher—they actually taught cooking to kids back in those days—and a Cordon Bleu-level cook. There is no doubt my interest in food and cooking came from her. Mum also comes from a big farming family and so was accustomed to there always being extra mouths to feed. She never batted an eyelid when we all appeared home with a friend—she would always manage to produce a meal to amply feed us all without the slightest fuss.

Her lasagne was one of our favourite meals—actually it still is. This was what she'd cook for our parties when there were would be 20-odd people around the table. I think her secret is the different cheeses, no other lasagne I've had can beat it. The Gateau Diane was her dinner party finale and we would hide in the kitchen hoping for leftovers. It takes some time and effort to make, but it is the most decadent, delicious dessert—I had Mum make it for my wedding cake! Mum has made her own marmalade every year for as long as I can remember. It always seems to be a little different each year so Dad gives her a rating out of 10 each time! Store bought is just not the same.

Lasagne

I use Philly cream, cottage cheese, grated mozzarella, emmental and cheddar for the selection of cheeses. Serve with a big green salad.

1 packet of fresh lasagne sheets (or you can substitute dried lasagne)

selection of cheeses

BOLOGNESE
1½ kg premium lean beef mince
2 medium-sized onions
2–3 large cloves garlic
1 red capsicum
1 orange/yellow capsicum
1 green capsicum
250–300 g mushrooms
pinch sea salt
lots of freshly ground black pepper

1 tsp oregano
1 tsp dill
1 tbsp paprika
1 bay leaf
140 g can tomato paste
400 g can chopped tomatoes
good glug red wine (or stock)

CHEESE SAUCE
120 g butter
120 g plain flour
1 litre milk

120 g grated cheddar cheese
salt, pepper and a little mustard

To make the bolognese, brown the mince in a large pan. It doesn't need any oil or fat. There is enough fat in the meat to do the job. Chop up the onions, garlic and capsicums and add into the browning mince. Slice the mushrooms and add. Season with salt and pepper, add all the spices, the tomato paste and tomatoes and stir well. Pour in a good glug of wine. Put to a gentle simmer and let it cook for about

40 minutes. You can't actually overcook it, so don't worry. Allow it to cool slightly before putting the whole dish together.

To make the cheese sauce, melt the butter, add the flour and cook for a few minutes without letting it colour. Gradually add the milk, stirring the whole time. Bring to the boil and cook for 4–5 minutes. Add the cheese and stir until it's all melted in, then season with salt, pepper and a little mustard.

Preheat the oven to 180°C.

Choose a large deep-sided casserole dish and assemble the lasagne as follows:

Layer 1: bolognese
Layer 2: lasagne sheets
Layer 3: little dollops of philly and cottage cheese
Layer 4: bolognese
Layer 5: lasagne sheets
Layer 6: grated mozzarella
Layer 7: bolognese
Layer 8: lasagne sheets
Layer 9: grated emmental
Layer 10: bolognese
Layer 11: lasagne sheets
Layer 12: cheese sauce.

Sprinkle some cheese over the top. (You can freeze it at this stage.) Bake in the preheated oven for about an hour. Serve with a large green salad.

Serves 14–16

Gateau Diane

This can easily be made well beforehand and frozen. It can then be eaten more or less straight from the freezer. It includes an unusual (for today) ingredient—camp coffee. This is a thick liquid and it comes in a bottle. Essentially it is a chicory and coffee essence and is used a lot in baking to flavour cakes, biscuits, puddings, meringues and cream.

MERINGUE
4 egg whites
225 g caster sugar

3 tsp instant coffee

CHOCOLATE CREAM
225 g butter
½ cup cold water
225 g sugar
4 egg yolks

120 g dessert chocolate
1 tbsp camp coffee
chocolate vermicelli or grated
    dark chocolate, to top

Preheat the oven to 150°C. Prepare 4 pieces of waxed paper marking an 18-cm diameter circle on each.

To make the meringue, beat egg whites until stiff. Add half the sugar and continue beating, add the remainder of sugar and coffee and beat again until stiff. Divide the mixture and spread evenly over the circles on the four pieces of waxed paper (sprinkling a little sugar on top if you like). Turn the oven down to around 80°C and place the meringues in the oven, leaving them in there overnight.

To make the chocolate cream, beat the butter until soft. Put water and sugar to boil—dissolve the sugar first and then boil rapidly for 2–5 minutes until a short thread forms at the end of a skewer.

Meantime beat the yolks until creamy. Pour the syrup very gradually over the yolks, beating continuously until thick and creamy. Beat in the butter. Melt the chocolate and coffee and beat in to the mixture. Keep in the fridge for 2–3 hours until thick but still spreadable.

Spread evenly between the meringues and coat the top as well. Sprinkle either chocolate vermicelli or grated dark chocolate over the top.

Serves 10

Mum's Marmalade

*Mum uses half jam sugar—that's the one with pectin already absorbed
into the sugar—and half either granulated or preserving sugar.*

1 kg Seville oranges
3.5 litres water

2 lemons
sugar

Wash the fruit, cut in half and squeeze out the juice into a jam pan.
Retain the pips and put them into a wee muslin bag or one of your old
knee-high stockings. Measure out the water into a container. Use some
it to cover the pips to soften and release the pectin. You'll get a jelly-
like substance after a few hours.

Chop up the squeezed fruit roughly into eighths. Liquidise a little at a
time with the water. (If you use a food processor instead of a liquidiser
then the pulp will be rougher.) Put the whole lot into the jam pan
along with the juice. If you like rind in your marmalade then before
cutting the fruit up grate some rind off and put into a wee pan, add a
little of the measured water and simmer to soften. Retain the rind and
pop the water back into the main pan. You can leave the jam at this
stage overnight, but I have done the whole thing in one go and it
makes little difference if the soaking of the seeds is missed out! Bring
the pulp, with the pips dangling inside the pot, to a boil and simmer
for 15–20 minutes. Allow to cool slightly so that there is no scalding at
the next stage!

Measure the pulp and add the sugar, allowing 560 g (1¼ lb) sugar to
each pint (600 ml) of pulp. Dissolve the sugar and bring all to the boil.
Keep it at a rolling boil for around 20 minutes. Test if ready by putting
a little onto a freezing saucer, leave for 2 minutes. Push your finger
through it and if a skin has formed then it's ready. Stir well and pot.

Makes 26 jars

Stefano Manfredi and his mother, Franca Manfredi

If I had to name my favourite dishes, they would not be those eaten at the many great restaurants I've had the pleasure of visiting around the world. No, they would all be dishes I remember having been prepared by my mother, Franca. Her tortelli di zucca (pumpkin tortellini) are the best I've eaten, though whenever I'm in the area of my birth in Italy I seek out new contenders. None have come close.

Tortelli di zucca (pumpkin tortelli) are a labour of love. From a large pumpkin, all the water has to be meticulously squeezed out until all that's left is a handful of concentrated bright yellow-orange flesh. Then a medieval miscellany of sweet, savoury and spice-laden ingredients is added. It's a dish Franca learnt from her mother Angelina and it's a tradition that I keep.

We began working together in our first restaurant, Restaurant Manfredi, in Sydney in 1983. Franca and I worked together for 20 years until 2002. From my mother I learnt dedication, sacrifice and tenacity for the craft of cooking.

Lattughe

Crostoli, chiacchere, risòle, galani, sassole, carafoi, puttanelle, frottole, nastrini, lattughe, or whatever Italians call them, are traditionally eaten during the Christmas season. They are festive-looking with their snow-white dusting, and they are utterly delicious.

5 eggs, separated
50 g caster sugar
40 g butter
30 ml grappa
grated rind of a lemon
juice of a lemon

750 g plain flour
1 tbsp baking powder
duck fat (preferably) or olive oil
    for frying
icing sugar

Beat the egg yolks, sugar and butter together. Mix in the grappa and the lemon rind and juice.

Whisk the egg whites till they form soft peaks and fold into the mixture. Add the flour and the baking powder and work in until you have a smooth dough.

Roll out into thin sheets using a pasta machine or rolling pin and cut into strips 8–10 cm long and 3 cm wide.

Heat the duck fat (or olive oil) in a pan. It's hot enough when a piece of the pastry sizzles instantly once dropped in. Gently tie each pastry into a loose knot before frying in the oil. Turn each once till they're golden brown. Drain on some absorbent paper.

When cool, dust with icing sugar and serve. They keep well in an airtight container stored in a cool pantry, not in the fridge.

Makes 40

Gnocchi with Burnt Butter and Sage

eLOGDL

The potatoes you use for this are very important. Older potatoes are best—generally speaking, choose potatoes that are not new season.

1.5 kg potatoes
300 g plain flour
50 g parmesan, grated
2 egg yolks
salt and pepper

pinch nutmeg
200 g butter
sage leaves
extra grated parmesan for
   serving

Brush the potatoes under cold water to remove the dirt and place them in a pot with 3–4 cm of water. Place a lid on the pot, bring to the boil and turn down to a simmer for 25–30 minutes until the potatoes are tender. Drain the cooked potatoes and let them cool a little. Remove their skins and mash them using a *schiacciapatate* (ricer) onto a work surface.

Make a well in the centre of the potato pile and add the flour, parmesan and egg yolks. Season with 3 good pinches of salt and some fine pepper and the nutmeg. Bring the lot together using your hands. If the dough seems a little sticky, add more flour.

Test by rolling a piece of the dough into a small sausage, about 3 cm thick, on a floured work surface and cutting some gnocchi about 2 cm wide. Bring a small pot of salted water to the boil and plunge in a couple of the gnocchi. Once they rise to the surface (60–90 seconds) remove with a slotted spoon and place on a plate. They should be firm but tender. If they are falling apart they need a little more flour in the mix.

Now shape the rest of your gnocchi and place them on a tray lined with a clean cloth. They can be made 3–4 hours ahead but no more.

To serve, poach the gnocchi in plenty of boiling water until they come up to the surface. Scoop them out with a slotted spoon and plate them.

Meanwhile, place the butter on high heat in a small pot until it has gone a nut-brown colour. At this stage, turn off the heat, add the sage to the burnt butter, sprinkle the gnocchi with some grated parmesan then spoon the sizzling butter over the lot. Serve immediately.

Serves 8 as a first course

Lyndey Milan and her mother, Isabel Hall

My mother was a good home cook. A woman of her time, she loved her garden and always cooked for her family and loved ones. My dad, Bill, would say that 'Mum's baked dinner is better than any fancy restaurant', even though they went out to one once a month with friends, which I thought at the time was just so glamorous—especially Mum's black suede heels.

What they taught my three siblings and me, more than anything, was the hospitality of the table. There was always room for another, and another, at our table. Should unexpected guests drop by, Mum could always conjure up something. All ages sat together, something continued with their beloved grandchildren. Dad would bring home business guests, people from overseas whom a friend or acquaintance had sent, and we sat at the table and talked with them. They all became firm friends. How could they not with such hospitality? Young people from overseas were not only fed, but

housed and shown the natural beauty of Sydney, of which Mum was so proud.

Dad was a senior executive so he worked late, but then he always came straight home. Dinner waited for him and we all ate together for as long as I, the youngest, can remember. Certainly I was hungry, and waiting for it and hoped he would get home before 7 pm and the ABC news on TV!

On our family boat, Mum's inventiveness came to the fore. She would save the empty plastic containers from candied honey. These would be filled with dessert made from whipped evaporated milk and half set jelly folded through with crushed pineapple and topped with whipped cream and nuts—a mystery for children on the boat who would have to dig down from the top to see what was underneath.

At Christmas, my parents would throw a big party for over 60 people. Mum of course did all the cooking, as she did subsequently for twenty-firsts and engagement parties. Didn't all mums? Chicken a la king, salmon in white sauce, her famous fried rice … Dad made the asparagus rolls, kept fresh under shredded lettuce and damp tea towels in the fridge, and Mum made pavlova, legendary fruit cake, chocolate log and white Christmas. Mum bought little gifts for everyone, Dad wrote ditties about them and dressed up as Santa and gave them out. Dad and his friends would put on skits, my Aunty would do her spoof on the little girl's first ballet concert, 'the picnic', and all was well with the world.

My kids would always walk in to their grandparents' place and look in the fridge—cottage cheese was a favourite, but nothing could beat Grandma's bran loaf.

Tomato and Onion Curry Sauce

Mum served this with steak for her and Dad, and lamb chops for the kids.

1 medium onion, peeled and
   quartered
1 tbsp oil or butter
1 tbsp curry powder
1 medium tomato, quartered

1 tbsp water
1 tbsp malt vinegar
1 tsp sugar
salt and pepper

Sauté onion in a little oil or butter till softened. Add the curry powder and continue sautéing a minute more. Add the tomato, water, vinegar, sugar and seasoning, and cook gently for 5 minutes or until tomato begins to break down. Serve with meat and three veg, of course!

Serves 2

Chocolate Log

This can also be made with ginger nut biscuits and apricot jam or ginger marmalade then sprinkled with chopped glace ginger. It's better made a couple of days ahead, though the chocolate may bleed through a little.

300 ml cream
vanilla essence
1 tsp caster sugar
1 packet plain (not coated)
  chocolate biscuits

2–3 tbsp sherry
raspberry jam
chocolate sprinkles

Make a 'Chantilly cream' by beating the cream with vanilla and sugar.

Sprinkle the biscuits with sherry. Spread the biscuits alternately, one with jam and the next with cream, until you have finished the packet. Sandwich the biscuits together into a log shape. When finished, cover the 'log' with the remaining whipped cream. Cover and refrigerate. As the colour from the biscuits can come through, cover with more cream just before serving. Shake over chocolate sprinkles and enjoy.

Coconut Cake

I remember coconut cake for birthdays or a cake covered with marshmallows and chocolate, or perhaps one in the shape of an 'L' as both my sisters' names and mine started with that letter.

Mum's recipe says 'ice the cake in layers'. This means let each thin layer of icing set before you give it another one—a bit like doing several coats of nail polish.

120 g butter
1 cup milk
½ cup desiccated coconut
vanilla essence

2 cups self-raising flour
1 cup sugar
pinch salt
1 egg

ICING
½ cup milk
1½ cups sugar
30 g butter

1 cup desiccated coconut
a few drops cochineal (red food
    colouring)

Preheat the oven to 180°C. Grease a small ring tin with butter.

Melt the butter in a saucepan and add the milk, coconut, and a few drops vanilla essence. In a large bowl, sift the flour, sugar and salt. Add the saucepan mixture to the bowl mixture and beat for a few minutes. Add the unbeaten egg and mix. Bake in a ring tin on the second bottom shelf of the oven for approximately 45 minutes.

For the icing, bring the milk to the boil. Remove from heat; add sugar. Stir over gentle heat till dissolved, then allow to boil gently for 8 minutes. Remove from heat. After a few minutes, add the butter, coconut and a few drops of cochineal. Beat well. It will thicken gradually. Ice the cake in layers.

Roberta Muir and her mother, Joan Muir

Growing up in the 1960s and 1970s in Anglo-Saxon Sydney suburbia, home-cooked meals were the norm, take-away (confined to the local Chinese restaurant) was rare, and dining out in restaurants unheard of. Dad worked night shift, and so wasn't often home for meals, but Mum made sure that we four children sat to the table every night for a balanced meat and three veg. Salads were popular in summer, platters of cold meat, tomato, cucumber, iceberg lettuce, grated carrot and hard-boiled eggs (no dressing), and Sunday evening was always a baked dinner (which I've never mastered), usually leg of lamb, shoulder of pork or large chicken with mounds of baked potatoes, pumpkin and carrot, mashed potato, boiled peas and beans and broccoli and cauliflower in cheese sauce. This was the most festive meal of the week and a time when Nanna or our school friends would often join us.

Crumbed Pan-fried Whiting with Baked Chips and Herb Mayonnaise

Fish featured heavily in our diet as Dad was a keen fisherman, always coming home from a day on the Hawkesbury River with bags of whiting, leatherjacket and bream.

½ cup extra virgin olive oil
4 potatoes, peeled and cut into bite-sized chunks
8 × 75 g whiting fillets, skin off

HERB MAYONNAISE
2 tbsp chopped gherkins
2 tbsp salted capers, rinsed and dried
2 tbsp finely chopped dill
2 tbsp finely chopped flat-leaf parsley

salt flakes and freshly ground black pepper, to taste
3 eggs, lightly beaten
3 cups fine breadcrumbs

2 tbsp finely chopped chervil
salt flakes and freshly ground black pepper, to taste
1 cup whole-egg mayonnaise

Preheat the oven to 200°C. For the baked chips, pour half the olive oil into a baking dish and place in the oven. Dry the potatoes well on absorbent paper. When the oil is hot, remove the dish, add the potatoes, stir well to coat and return to the oven for 45–60 minutes, until crisp and brown, stirring occasionally.

To make the mayonnaise, combine all the ingredients and set aside in the fridge.

To cook the fish, sprinkle each whiting fillet generously with salt and pepper on both sides. Dip fish in egg, then in breadcrumbs, gently pressing the crumbs onto the fish. Repeat egg and breadcrumb process then cover and refrigerate until ready to cook.

Heat the remaining oil in a large frying pan over medium heat when the potatoes are nearly ready. When hot, add the fish and cook the fillets for about 1 minute each side, until golden, then drain on paper towel. Rather than crowding the pan, cook the fish in batches if need be.

Remove the potatoes from oven, drain on paper towel, place in a warmed serving bowl and salt well. Serve the fish with the mayonnaise, the potatoes and a green salad.

Serves 4

Mum's Chocolate, Cherry and Almond Cake

Once we all went to school, Mum went back to work and time was at a premium. During these years, packet cake mixes became a necessary evil, but I never thought the insubstantial creations they produced were a patch on the cakes Mum used to make. Thankfully, since she's retired, she's gone back to the old ways and also started experimenting with new cakes such as her now famous Chocolate, Cherry and Almond Cake. It's become such a hit with everyone who tries it that she often spends days baking batches of them to distribute to family and friends. The almond meal makes it very moist so it keeps well—though it rarely lasts that long.

750 g preserved sour cherries
200 g salted butter, softened
1 cup caster sugar
4 eggs
100 g almond meal

100 g dark chocolate, grated
2 tbsp rum
1 cup self-raising flour, sifted
1 tsp ground cinnamon
⅓ cup flaked almonds

Preheat the oven to 160°C. Grease a deep, 25-cm round spring pan and line the base with baking paper.

Drain the cherries on absorbent paper or, even better, overnight in a colander.

Beat the butter and sugar in a large bowl with an electric mixer until light and fluffy. Add the eggs, one at a time, beating on low speed between additions so the eggs are just combined.

Using a wooden spoon, stir in the almond meal, chocolate, rum, flour, cinnamon and half the flaked almonds, then the cherries.

Pour the mixture into the prepared pan, sprinkle the remaining flaked almonds on top and bake for about 1 hour and 10 minutes, until a wooden skewer comes out dry when inserted into the centre. If the top of the cake browns too much while cooking, cover the pan loosely with foil. Stand for 5 minutes before turning out onto a wire rack. Serve warm or cold.

Home-made treats

'The table was a noisy place and friends from smaller families, not used to talking over the top of someone else in order to have their say, were often quite perplexed by the cacophony. We weren't big dessert eaters, but Sunday was the exception when my Nanna's clove-studded apple pie reigned supreme, with home-made custard or shop-bought ice-cream—usually both.

While we didn't eat a lot of desserts, there were always home-baked cakes, biscuits and slices for our lunch boxes and to have with a cup of tea. My earliest food memory is watching Mum cream butter and sugar with a wooden spoon to make a simple butter cake and whisk egg whites with an old rotary hand-beater for the super-light sponges that were filled with strawberry jam and whipped cream as birthday cakes.'

John Newton and his mother, Gloria Newton

My mother shaped my interest in food by both her adventurous (for the times) cooking and by dragging me in my short pants school uniform to some very flash restaurants (again, for the times). I thank her, from the bottom of my stomach.

When my father died (21 years after my mother) I discovered a number of her recipes in his apartment. They were typed out on little rectangular sheets of the copy paper that journalists used to use when they wrote their stories on typewriters.

When I visited my mother at *The Daily Mirror*, I remember her sitting behind a giant black typewriter, a Remington I think it was, on her right a pile of copy paper. The way they wrote stories in those days was to roll two sheets of copy paper separated by a carbon paper into the machine, and tap it out one paragraph at a time. When the story was finished, a copy boy ('COPY BOY!' she yelled) would take the pile of copy paper down to the editor and then to the compositor's room when it was edited. It made sense.

If you wanted to change one paragraph, you didn't have to re-write the whole page. If you wanted to add a para, ditto. It also put a limit to the length of a paragraph.

So when Mum sat between stories at her typewriter, she'd sometimes roll in a sheet of copy paper, and type out a recipe. Where did she get them? I have no idea. Some, because she was a restaurant writer—she ran a column called 'Goings on About Town' under the by-line Elizabeth Pitt—probably came from restaurateurs or chefs. Others may have been plucked from the *Women's Weekly* (where she later worked).

I vaguely remember eating some of them—Spaghetti and Meatballs Napoli, although I doubt very much whether we ever called it Napoli, and Shrimp and Crabmeat au Gratin ring a bell. She loved a good gratin my mum, almost as much as she loved a mould—tuna and salmon mousse were her favourites, using tinned fish of course. She had a fish-shaped anodised aluminium mould, and would tip the big blobby gelatined mould onto a large plate at buffet dinners. She also loved a buffet dinner.

There was no recipe for salmon mousse in the collection—she probably did it from memory. She may have used one from Margaret Fulton's columns or perhaps from the old *Australian Women's Weekly Cookbook*, edited by Ellen Sinclair whose photo in the book, with frosted, heavily sprayed and carefully coiffed hair, reminds me of my dear old Mum who died, sadly, of breast cancer.

Salmon Mousse with Sour Cream Dressing

I found this one on page 286 of the Margaret Fulton Cookbook. *According to Margaret, she was given the recipe by a very distinguished English cook. It must have been a global standard in the seventies: certainly it looks very similar to my mum's mousse although Margaret used flaked red salmon which could conceivably be fresh rather than tinned as it was back then.*

1 tbsp powdered gelatine
¼ cup water
2 tsp sugar
1 tsp salt
1 tsp dry mustard
¼ cup white wine vinegar

2 cups flaked red salmon
1 cup finely diced celery
2 tsp capers
½ cup whipped cream
a few sprigs of dill, to garnish

SOUR CREAM DRESSING
½ cup sour cream
1 tbsp grated onion
½ tsp salt
freshly ground black pepper

1 tsp grated horseradish relish
  (optional)
2 tsp white wine vinegar
1 pinch of paprika

Sprinkle the gelatine over the water in a small saucepan. Soak for 2 minutes. Add the sugar, salt, mustard and vinegar. Stir constantly over a low heat until the gelatine is dissolved. Remove from the heat and chill to the consistency of unbeaten egg whites.

Fold in the salmon, celery and capers, mix well, then fold in the whipped cream. Turn into a wetted 4-cup mould or 8 individual moulds, and chill until firm.

Unmould onto a serving plate and garnish with sprigs of fresh dill. Serve with the sour cream dressing.

To make the sour cream dressing, combine all the ingredients in a bowl.

Serves 8

Poires au Vin

Poached Pears

This recipe is very little changed—except for the arrowroot—from the way I would make it today, although I might occasionally substitute mascarpone for the cream. A pint in those days was 568 ml, so allowing a bit over 1 metric cup for a ½ pint will be about right.

6 cooking pears, hard
120 g sugar
½ pint water
½ pint red wine

2.5 cm cinnamon stick
small strip of lemon rind
arrowroot

Peel pears, leaving whole with stalks on. Put into baking dish with sugar, water, wine, cinnamon and lemon. Cover and cook gently in slow oven until tender. Serve piled up in a compotier with a stand. Boil the wine syrup until reduced by half, then thicken with a little arrowroot and pour over the pears. Serve with a jug of cream.

Serves 6

Dining out

⌒⌒⌒⌒

I have many food memories of my life with Gloria. One of my earliest—and surely given my later profession, most formative—was of dining at a restaurant called Rainaud's which was, I'm pretty sure, at the top of King Street near Macquarie Street, where the Law Courts now are in Sydney. It used to be called Queen's Square after the statue of an imposing Victoria opposite an adoring Albert, later moved to the Queen Victoria Building.

I remember little of the food, but recall being terribly impressed with the weight of the cutlery, knobbly silver stuff, and the thick, white starched table cloth—double damask I'll bet. Dad used to disappear into a back room with (was it Jim?) Rainaud who, despite the name, was as Greek as the Parthenon, and they'd sit and drink brandy and smoke Craven A cigarettes under the gallery of race horses on the wall. Rainaud owned a stable of race horses, and Dad was always a sucker for the horses.

Armando Percuoco and his mother, Olimpia Percuoco

When I was growing up in Naples, my parents followed a division of labour that proved very useful to me in later life. My father did the shopping and my mother did the cooking.

I would go to the markets with Dad and watch him choose the freshest fish, the fruits, vegetables and leaves that were at their seasonal best, and the tastiest cuts for our modest budget. Back home I'd join my brothers and sisters in helping Mum turn those ingredients into sauces, salads and stews and desserts. Then we would sit down to a family meal full of big flavours and loud conversation.

Buon appetito.

Scaloppine alla Caprese

This classic Italian dish was supposedly invented on the island of Capri. I am very attached to Capri, not only because it is a romantic island in the gulf of Naples, but also because I worked at Canzone del Mare when I was very young. I made a lot of friends there, some of whom I rediscovered in the same business when I arrived in this country.

16 thin slices of veal, each about 50 g
plain flour, for dipping
2 tbsp olive oil, plus extra for frying
2 medium eggplants, each cut crosswise into 8 slices ½ cm thick

16 slices of mozzarella
bunch basil
1 tbsp butter
¼ cup Napoletana sauce (see recipe page 112)
¼ cup dry white wine

Spread plastic wrap over the meat slices and gently beat them with a mallet or small rolling pin until they spread out to about double their original size. Dip the pieces in flour, being careful to coat both sides. Heat 2 tablespoons of olive oil in a frying pan over medium heat and sauté the veal for about 2 minutes on each side. Lay them in a large flameproof dish or clean frying pan in a single layer.

Pour olive oil into a deep frying pan to a depth of about 5 cm and heat until it sizzles when a drop of water is thrown in. Fry the eggplant slices until they are golden, about 3 minutes. Drain them on paper towels.

Lay a slice of eggplant on each piece of veal then top with a slice of mozzarella, 2 basil leaves and finally a dab of butter. Pour the Napoletana sauce and wine around the scaloppini. Simmer over a low heat for 5 minutes, basting with the juices in the pan.

To serve, put 4 scaloppine on each plate. Reduce the remaining liquid in the pan over high heat for 1 minute then pour the sauce over the scaloppine. Serve with roast potatoes and green beans.

Serves 4

Napoletana sauce

Every household in Naples has oil, garlic, tomatoes and a bunch of fresh basil as part of their basic kitchen supplies, so they can throw together a Napoletana sauce at any time. The sauce can go on pasta or pizza or a piece of fish just as it is. You can make this sauce in 12 minutes and any that's left over can be kept for a couple of days in the fridge.

1 clove garlic
3 tbsp olive oil
400 g tomatoes, chopped
  (canned are fine)

10 basil leaves, chopped
salt

Thump a clove of garlic with the heel of your hand, remove the skin and sauté it in a saucepan with the olive oil over high heat for about 2 minutes until it turns golden. Add 400 g chopped tomatoes and cook uncovered over medium heat for 8 minutes. Add the chopped basil leaves and simmer for another 2 minutes. Taste and add salt as necessary. Remove the garlic clove.

This makes about 2 cups of sauce.

Broccoli di rape

Although northern Italians don't use much chilli, we like it in the south because it seems to match our climate.

2 bunches broccoli di rape
6 tbsp olive oil
2 cloves garlic, peeled

1 small red chilli
salt and pepper

To prepare broccoli di rape, remove and discard the stems. Wash the leaves well and pat them dry with paper towel.

In a flameproof casserole dish, heat 3 tablespoons of the oil and add the garlic cloves. Cook until the garlic just turns brown. Split the chilli in half, remove and discard the seeds and add it to the oil. Add the rape leaves and mix a little over a high heat. Cover with the lid, reduce the heat to medium and cook gently for 30 minutes. Add salt to your taste and serve as a side dish with pork or sausages. The bitterness of the vegetable will cut the fat in the meat.

Serves 4

Pere Olimpia
Spiced Pears in White Wine

My mother used to cook this for us in Italy and we introduced it into our restaurant, Pulcinella, when we opened it in 1979.

4 brown pears, fairly firm and
    unpeeled
4 tbsp sugar
2 cups white wine

3 tsp ground cinnamon
4 cloves
whipped cream to serve

Preheat the oven to 180°C.

Wash the pears and place them in an ovenproof dish. Add the sugar, wine, cinnamon and cloves, and cover the dish with foil. Bake in the preheated oven for 20 minutes. Remove from the oven and allow to cool. Drain the pears, reserving the cooking liquid.

Bring the liquid to the boil in a small pan and cook over high heat until reduced by about one third. It should be of a thick consistency.

To serve, put a pear on each plate, add a dollop of whipped cream and drizzle over the sauce.

Damien Pignolet and his mother, Elsa Pignolet

My mother, Elsa, lived for her family. Apart from the care she offered individually to each child, Mum's real love was expressed through her delicious food.

She was born to cook, although not in the way we talk about cooks today. What she had as a primary tool was her fine palate and an overwhelming wish to please her family and guests.

Elsa's gentle, nurturing cooking led me to become a cook.

Elsa Pignolet's Split Pea Soup

My mother Elsa was a brilliant soup cook, as she served soup as the first course for virtually every evening meal. She liked to use a pressure cooker since she believed all the nutrients were retained for the health of the family. Pressure cooking is ideal for pulses because of the speedy results. Here is a traditional cooking method however, as not many people use a pressure cooker these days. Elsa didn't make croutons for this, but I like the texture they provide.

1 large onion, diced finely
1–2 carrots, peeled and diced finely
1 celery stalk, diced finely
1–2 tbsp bacon fat or vegetable oil
500 g yellow split peas, rinsed well and soaked overnight in cold water

1 ham hock
2–3 litres cold water, enough to cover the ingredients well
1 bay leaf
salt to taste
freshly ground white pepper
chopped parsley

CROUTONS (OPTIONAL)
3–4 × 1-cm thick slices of white bread (crusts removed)

vegetable oil

Use a 5-litre pot to cook the diced vegetables in the bacon fat or oil until soft; but don't brown them. Drain the peas, rinse again and add to the vegetables with the ham hock and water but no salt. Bring to the boil, skim the surface then add the bay leaf and simmer, partially covered, for about 1 hour or until the peas are really soft. Discard the bay leaf.

Remove the hock and dice the flesh (and the skin if liked) into small pieces. Puree the soup with the liquid in batches either through a food mill or in a blender and season to taste with salt and pepper. Reheat before serving, stirring constantly, and serve with the ham hock and chopped parsley.

For the croutons, dice the bread into 1-cm pieces and fry in hot oil until golden. Drain on paper towel. Scatter over the soup at the last moment.

Makes about 8 good serves

Grandmother Morgan's Field Mushrooms

Cultivated mushrooms simply cannot compare in juiciness, colour, texture and intensity of flavour with field mushrooms. If you have access to naturally growing field mushrooms, please try this recipe—it will transport you to another era. Grandmother Morgan's recipe might seem outrageously heavy on the butter by today's standards, but the taste and texture will suffer without it. If you are concerned about your intake of fat, just eat a small helping. This recipe is from my book, French.

450 g bacon, rind removed and
  roughly chopped
450 g unsalted butter
600 g fresh field mushrooms, cut
  into 1-cm thick slices

salt and pepper
plenty of freshly chopped
  parsley

In a large frying pan with a lid, cook the bacon in a few tablespoons of the butter over slow heat until the fat melts, but do not let it fry.

Add the rest of the butter and, when it has melted, add the mushrooms, seasoning them with salt and pepper.

Put the lid on the pan and allow the mushrooms to sweat until they begin to soften, stirring occasionally so that they cook evenly.

Remove the lid and cook until the mushrooms are soft and the liquid slightly thickened. Check the seasoning and stir in the parsley.

Serves 4—or many more!

Mushroom gathering

'During my childhood the family would drive some 45 km from home to the Dandenong Ranges, to a lovely place opposite the forest. On the way, beyond the market gardens, lay open fields where the true field mushrooms grew in abundance in autumn. Armed with a basket we would collect these treasures and return with blackened fingers to the car, which took on the intense earthy aroma of the 'mushies', as we called them. The first job on arrival at our house opposite Sherbrook Forest in Belgrave, Victoria, was to light the fuel stove ready for a mushroom fry-up, using my grandmother's recipe and served on old-fashioned white-bread toast.'

Jan Purser and her mother, Shirley Purser

Growing up as the youngest of three girls in a typical 1960s suburban family in Sydney was fun. I remember water fights with Dad in the backyard with us all ganging up on him and Mum laughing hysterically as she watched us getting soaked. She has always had an infectious loud laugh. Mum's cooking was typical of the time. She and Dad were busy juggling work with family so we had basic, simple and nutritious fare most of the time with special dishes for birthdays and other occasions.

I started cooking at the age of nine and began with cupcakes. Life took on a whole new (sweet) meaning for me then, and every weekend I would make biscuits, slices, cakes and pies galore. Mum's kitchen rules were I had to wash up and clean up everything once I'd finished. Looking back I think Mum was great for giving me the run of the kitchen, always encouraging me to explore new recipes and cook dinner as often as I liked. Mum and the rest of the family probably suffered a little from my experiments in those days but I don't recall any complaints. Bless them!

Shirley's Meatloaf

Meatloaf is such great comfort food and it was a regular on the menu in the 1960s and 1970s at our place. We had mince about once a week, either cooked into a meatloaf, Bolognese sauce with spaghetti or rissoles. I cook Mum's meatloaf often these days and love having it with good-quality chutney or relish and a crisp salad.

1 tbsp oil
1 brown onion, finely chopped
2 bacon rashers, finely chopped
(optional)
5 slices bread, crusts removed
¾ cup milk
1 kg good quality lean minced
beef

2 eggs
50 g sachet tomato paste
1 tbsp bottled horseradish
cream (optional)
1 tsp salt
freshly ground black pepper

Preheat the oven to 180°C.

Heat the oil in frying pan over medium heat and sauté onion and bacon until the onion is soft. Set aside to cool.

Cut the bread into cubes and place in a bowl. Pour the milk over the top and leave to soak until the milk is absorbed.

Combine the onion mixture, bread mixture, mince, eggs, tomato paste, horseradish cream, salt and pepper in a large bowl and mix well.

Spoon the mixture into an oiled loaf pan and smooth the surface. Bake the meatloaf in the preheated oven for 50–60 minutes, or until it is cooked through. Let it stand for 5–10 minutes before cutting into slices to serve. Serve hot with vegetables or cold with chutney and salad.

Serves 6–8

Apricot Roll

～～～

Mum's desserts really stand out in my childhood memories, because I inherited my paternal grandfather's insatiable sweet tooth. One of my favourites is Mum's apricot roll. The tartness of the apricots complements the caramel sweetness of the sauce. A great combination and it really satisfies that sweet tooth!

PASTRY
80 g butter
170 g self-raising flour
¼ cup water, approximately

1 cup dried apricot halves,
    soaked overnight in water
milk, for glazing

SAUCE
½ cup golden syrup
½ cup water

½ cup brown sugar

Preheat the oven to 200°C.

To make the pastry, rub the butter into the flour until it looks like breadcrumbs. Make a well in the centre. Pour almost all the water in and use a round-bladed knife to cut through the mixture until the ingredients clump together to form a dry dough, adding the remaining water if needed. Knead lightly on a lightly floured surface until smooth. Use a rolling pin to roll the dough out on a lightly floured surface until 20 cm × 30 cm.

Drain the apricots well and arrange over the pastry in a single layer leaving the edges free. Brush a long edge of pastry with milk. Starting from the opposite long edge, roll up the pastry, enclosing the apricots, into a neat roll. Tuck under the ends. Place the roll, seam-side down, into a greased 20 cm × 30 cm ovenproof dish.

To make the sauce, combine the golden syrup, water and sugar in a small saucepan and stir over low heat until sugar dissolves. Bring to the boil then pour over the apricot roll in the dish. Bake in the preheated oven for 30–40 minutes, or until the pastry is browned and crisp. Serve sliced with custard and ice-cream.

Serves 6

Stewed Apples with Dumplings

This was one of my favourite winter desserts and I would request it for my birthday dinner dessert each year. The combination of comforting steamed dumplings and sweet apples with custard and ice-cream is simple and totally heart-warming.

6 Granny Smith apples, peeled, quartered

⅓ cup sugar

DUMPLINGS

2 cups self-raising flour
1 tbsp sugar

1 rounded tbsp (25 g) butter
¾ cup milk, approximately

Cut the apple quarters lengthways into thin slices (2 mm thick). Place the apples and sugar in a large saucepan. Add enough water to almost cover the apples.

To begin making the dumplings, combine the flour and sugar in a medium bowl and rub in the butter.

Bring the apples to the boil, reduce heat, cover and simmer for 7 minutes.

While the apples are cooking, finish the dumplings. Add the milk to the flour mixture and use a round-bladed knife to cut through and mix to a soft dough. Turn onto a lightly floured surface and knead very gently until just smooth underneath.

Using lightly floured hands, break dough evenly into 12 portions and roll each gently into a ball. Place the dumplings on top of the apples in a single layer, cover with the lid and cook for 15 minutes or so, or until the dumplings are cooked through when tested with a fork. Serve hot with custard and/or vanilla ice-cream.

Serves 6

Cherry Ripe and her mother, Joyce Dent

We were halfway through our roast Sunday lunch, my father waxing lyrical about the paleness of the milk-fed flesh: how of the three wethers he'd taken to the butcher, this was the carcass he had picked out for us.

It was my pet lamb, P12, which with my small wrist I had managed to extricate from its dying mother without suffocating it. It was so small it fitted into a shoebox kept in front of the Aga. First I hand-fed him with milk from an eye-dropper, then he guzzled milk through a cut-off teat of a baby's bottle. Put out to pasture with the flock, all through the summer he would come gambolling at the sound of my voice. Now he was here on my plate.

It was one of the hardest lessons I ever had to learn: what farmers do is raise animals to be eaten. While I was repulsed at the time, I came to appreciate that was the reason for the quality of food on our table. Every mealtime the conversation was about the ingredients: mother would not pick peas more than an hour before lunch as father could discern the difference.

Broad Beans in Parsley Sauce with Bacon

As a Sydney-born bride of an English farmer on the eve of World War II, Mother couldn't boil even an egg. By the time I came along, she had mastered heavenly choux pastry, the lightest angel sponge cakes, macaroons, tuiles and brandy snaps. Her dishes from the garden are legendary, and still spoken about reverentially by the family to this day, such as this Sunday night supper dish. In our kitchen garden the size of two tennis courts, parsley flourished. It is important to use nearly three times as much parsley as béchamel! Think of it as a warm salsa verde.

1 large bunch of curly (English) parsley (about 20 large stems)
5 rashers bacon, rinds removed
1.5 kg fresh broad beans, podded, or 500 g frozen
1½ tsp cultured butter
1½ tbsp plain flour
300 ml milk
1 tbsp white wine vinegar or apple cider vinegar, or more to taste

Destalk the parsley. Chop, or pulse slowly in food processor until very finely chopped but not pureed.

Grill the bacon until browned to crumble point. Drain between layers of paper towel.

Boil or steam the broad beans until soft. Set aside and keep warm. If using frozen broad beans, remove their outer skins after cooking.

Melt the butter in a heavy-based saucepan until all moisture has evaporated. Take off the heat, add the flour and stir vigorously until just turning colour. Back on the heat, add the milk little by little, stirring constantly to make a thick paste with no lumps until you have a smooth béchamel the consistency of custard. (If using a wand blender, add all the milk at once, and blend.)

Four minutes before serving, add the very finely chopped parsley. Bring back to the boil, constantly scraping the bottom of the saucepan so it doesn't catch. Taste to ensure the parsley is cooked. Take off the heat, and stir in the vinegar. Put it back on the heat, but do not allow to boil again, as it will curdle.

Divide the warm broad beans into individual bowls, pour over the parsley sauce, and crumble the crisp bacon on top. (Parmigiano reggiano shaved on top works a treat.)

Serves 4

Orange Flummery

My mother's original recipe came from her Country Women's Association Cookbook and hideously called for a boiled 'flour and water paste', cooled and whipped. Over the years, Mother's mutated into a creamy mousse using cream from our Jersey house cow. I have further adapted it to be suitable for people with diabetes.

Although I wasn't to realise it until three decades later, another significant moment in my childhood, which came to influence my food writing, occurred in the strawberry patch one summer evening when I was about nine. My father and I were picking strawberries for supper, and he was complaining bitterly that the only strawberry varieties available in the 1950s totally lacked the flavour of the varieties available in his boyhood, a bowlful of which would perfume an entire room. In the late 1980s, when evidence emerged of the massive reduction in domestic agricultural biodiversity and the disappearance (read 'extinction') of thousands of open-pollinated varieties of fruits and vegetables, I came to champion heritage or heirloom seeds which can be saved and re-planted, and which—unlike hybrid seeds from multinational seed companies—grow true-to-type. Since the mid-1990s, protecting food biodiversity has become a major focus of the Slow Food movement worldwide.

The orange flummery recipe can be made with a strawberry puree, but is relatively tasteless. It is best made with citrus fruit, as the genetic engineers and multinational seed companies haven't yet bred the flavour out of them!

2 oranges	10 g gelatine
1 lemon	2 egg whites
2 tsp sugar (or Splenda powder)	150 g low fat sour cream

Zest or score the skin of one of the oranges to very fine juliennes (strips).

Juice both oranges and the lemon, for 250 ml juice. Warm the juice. Take off the heat, add the sugar and gelatine and whisk to dissolve, warming if necessary without boiling to remove any lumps. Cool to room temperature, and whisk to aerate, and then stir in the cream until smooth.

Separately whisk the egg whites to stiff peaks and slowly incorporate the juice, gelatine and cream mixture. Pour into a glass serving bowl and refrigerate, covered. In winter, bring back to room temperature before serving.

To make it more contemporary, garnish with fresh berries, and serve with almond biscotti.

Serves 4

Philippa Sandall and her mother, Margie Norris

There was always lots of talk and laughter around the table as we sat down together every night at about 6.30. My mum was a good basic cook (until Elizabeth David's books arrived in New Zealand and transformed her repertoire with things like a 'daube'). She also had to deal with a family that doubled in size overnight—her beloved younger sister died of breast cancer and her three children lived with us for a couple of years along with my grandmother who helped out (and always seemed to be darning socks).

Feeding five children and three adults was 'stretch-the-budget', 'stick-to-the-ribs' fare—meat, three veg and a filling pudding from chocolate blancmange and junket to steamed pud and Krümeltorte (an apple crumble and regular opportunity, sister Ali remembers, for Dad to demonstrate how to pronounce the German 'ü').

We all had jobs to do. I often helped Mum prepare dinner—shelling peas, mashing potatoes, mincing the leftover lamb for shepherd's pie. I loved being in the kitchen and cooking and I loved that special time, just me with my mum.

Creamy Smoked Fish Pie with Mashed Potato Topping

∽⚯⚭∼

When I grew up in New Zealand, we always had fish on Fridays (it was really fresh on Fridays, Mum said). I loved this creamy pie she made with smoked snapper (it had no bones). When we were older she added capers to the pie. The milk she used was creamy-topped New Zealand whole milk; low-fat milk didn't exist. For a milder flavour you could make this with a mixture of smoked fish and fresh fish.

MASHED POTATO TOPPING

3–4 potatoes (about 750 g), peeled and cut into chunks

½ cup milk, warmed

salt and freshly ground black pepper

3 tbsp grated tasty cheese

WHITE SAUCE

2 tbsp butter

1 small onion, finely chopped

4 tbsp plain flour

2 cups milk, warmed

about 750 g smoked fish, flaked

¼ cup chopped parsley

1 tbsp lemon juice

Preheat the oven to 180°C.

To make the topping, cook the potatoes until tender then drain and mash them, beating in just enough warm milk for a creamy, smooth mash. Season with salt and pepper.

To make the sauce, heat the butter in a medium saucepan and sauté the onion over a low heat for about 5 minutes or until soft. Don't let it catch and burn. Stir in the flour with a wooden spoon, cook for a minute, then gradually stir (or whisk) in the milk. Bring to the boil, stirring frequently until the sauce is smooth and creamy. Remove from the heat, stir in the fish flakes, parsley and lemon juice, then taste and season with pepper if you wish.

Spoon the mixture into an ovenproof pie dish (Mum used an oblong Pyrex one) and spread the smashed potato evenly over the top. Run a fork through the mixture—this helps it go crusty, and this was the bit I loved to do. Top with grated cheese and bake for about 20 minutes or until bubbling and the top is golden brown.

Serves 4–6

Plum Jam

We had three plum trees in our garden—a greengage that we picked
and ate, a big crimson-fleshed, late-ripening plum that Mum bottled,
and an incredibly bumper-cropping 'Christmas' plum with purplish
red skin and yellow flesh that became pots and pots of plum jam and
plum chutney to eat or give away, and even some plum liqueur one
year. It was such a prolific producer we couldn't keep up, and plums
lay around fermenting on the ground (I can still smell them). One
year we rescued a tipsy thrush who had over-indulged—it took him
several hours to sober up.

2 kg firm, ripe plums without blemishes	1½ cups cold water
	7 cups sugar

Wash and dry the plums, cut in half and remove and discard the
stones.

Put the plums in a large, heavy-based preserving pan with the water,
bring to the boil and simmer gently until they are soft and pulpy.

Add the sugar, stirring until it is dissolved. Bring the mixture to a
'rolling boil' and boil for 15 minutes, skimming off any froth that forms
on the surface, then test for setting by placing a teaspoon of the
mixture on a chilled saucer. Let it cool. Run your finger through the
jam and if the surface wrinkles slightly and the jam stays in 2 separate
portions, it's bottling time.

Ladle the jam carefully into the sterilised jars and seal. Invert the jars
for about 30 seconds, then turn upright and set aside to cool. Label
when cold—Mum had lovely clear handwriting.

Mum oven-sterilised her jars. She washed them in hot soapy water,
rinsed them and then placed them upside down on a baking tray in a
150°C oven for about 30 minutes. Then she turned to oven off and left
the jars there until the jam was ready for bottling.

Makes about 8 cups

Good manners

Table manners were instilled in a fun sort of way—most of the time. Dad would say, "You won't get invited to 'GH' (Government House, the 'A' list of the olden days) if you put your elbows on the table." Other rules were to sit up straight, put your napkin on your lap, wait for everyone to be served before tucking in (saying Grace was a good way to make everyone wait), no stretching and spoon soup toward the far edge of the bowl. We also had to ask to be excused, and, more often than not, were told "no" since not everyone had finished eating.

Joanna Savill and her mother, Ann Savill

I am a firm believer that we connect with people who have the same feelings about food as we do, and that growing up with good food gives you an instinctive connection to eating and cooking. My mother spent endless time in the kitchen—lots of those 1970s dinner parties!—and my grandmother even more so, living on a sheep station and turning out breakfast, morning tea (or smoko), lunch, afternoon tea (another smoko) and dinner on a daily basis.

We ate well as kids, travelled a fair bit as a family and learned to be adventurous cooks. My sisters (four of us altogether) and I all have our specialties. Mum's include cheese biscuits, Christmas pudding and meringues. She is a meringue whizz, although she always downplays the result. 'A bit dry', 'a bit gooey', 'not quite right today'. It's rubbish, of course. She bakes perfect pavs too, lately using a Silpat (silicone sheet), which I bought for her. She swears by it. It's nice to think I've helped her pav along just a little.

Cheese Biscuits

This very simple recipe is an absolute staple in my mother's kitchen. We always search for the cheese biscuit jar in her pantry cupboard, usually within minutes of arriving at her house for family occasions. I started making them as a teenager when I was a very keen after-school baker. (I still love baking now.) I don't know where the recipe came from originally and Mum has now given up on the coconut option, which is probably very retro this days!

2 tbsp rice bubbles
180 g hard cheese, grated (tasty or vintage cheddar)
30 g parmesan, grated
180 g butter
salt and cayenne pepper and paprika and dry mustard, to taste
180 g plain flour
desiccated coconut (optional)

Preheat the oven to 180°C.

Place the rice bubbles in a mixing bowl and beat to crush. Set aside. Cream the cheeses and butter in a mixing bowl, then season with salt, cayenne pepper, paprika and dry mustard to taste. Fold in the flour and rice bubbles and knead to a dough.

Roll the dough into small balls. Roll in coconut if used. Place each ball on a baking tray lined with baking paper. Press biscuits down with a fork and bake for 12 to 15 minutes or until golden brown.

Oven-fried Chicken

This was our family picnic chicken. I think we found it a reasonable alternative to the 'secret herbs and spices' variety which we thought was so wonderful back in the 1970s. The recipe was adapted from Robert Carrier's Great Dishes of the World *(published in 1963). 'Very avant garde', says Mum. She would pack small baskets with paper serviettes in them so we could have chicken in a basket. I added the sage leaves because I love fresh sage with chicken.*

50 g plain flour
1 tsp salt
1 tsp pepper
1 tbsp chopped fresh parsley
1 tsp dried tarragon
1 tsp dried rosemary

1 bunch fresh sage leaves,
  roughly chopped
grated zest of a lemon
1 egg, beaten
milk
1 kg chicken pieces
6 tbsp olive oil

Combine the flour, salt, pepper, herbs and lemon zest in a bowl.

Beat the egg and milk together in a separate bowl.

Dip the chicken pieces into egg mixture and then into seasoned flour. Chill for about 10 minutes, while preheating the oven to 180°C.

Pour the oil into a shallow baking tray and heat in a moderate oven. Place the chicken pieces in the tray and turn them over to coat with the warm oil. Bake the pieces, turning occasionally, for approximately 45 minutes or until the chicken is cooked.

Serves 4

Easy Chocolate Fudge Cake

This one-pot chocolate cake is so easy. Mum says she got the recipe 'between hands at bridge'. The raisins give it gooey-ness but you could omit them, or use sultanas instead.

1½ cups water
1 cup raisins
250 g butter
1 cup sugar
½ tsp cinnamon
½ tsp ground cloves

3 tbsp cocoa powder
pinch salt
1 tsp bicarbonate of soda
¼ cup boiling water
2 cups plain flour, sifted

Preheat the oven to 180°C. Grease a 23-cm cake tin.

Place the water, raisins, butter, sugar, cinnamon, cloves, cocoa and salt in a large saucepan, bring to a boil then reduce the heat and simmer for 5 minutes. Remove and cool.

Dissolve the bicarbonate of soda in ¼ cup boiling water and add to the cooled mixture with the sifted plain flour.

Pour the mixture into the greased cake tin and bake for 30 minutes or until cooked. Cool in the tin. Dust with icing sugar or ice when turned out on rack.

Catherine Saxelby and her mother, Anne Switala

My mother Anne (Hanka in Polish) was a natural-born cook. She never used a recipe but cooked by eye, and years of experience. Her food always tasted delicious whether it was Polish fare like *bigos* or recipes she picked up from her friends as a 'New Australian' in Sydney in the 1950s. So I recall dinners of roasts or steaks kicked off with an appetiser of herring with onion and sour cream served with pumpernickel. Weird, but somehow it all tasted good.

She would enliven meals with those wonderful European delicacies such as best-quality Polish hams, sauerkraut and grated horseradish. Traditional Jewish dishes like cabbage rolls and gefilte fish were often on the table as we had a lot of Jewish friends—my mother co-owned a small business in the rag trade in Surry Hills making evening wear.

Desserts that stick in my taste-bud memory are her rich cheesecake with eggs, vanilla and sour cream and her thin crepes filled with the most delicious mix of farm cheese, currants and lemon rind, which I have included here.

CLOSE
SAFETY
BAR

Anne's Polish Potato Salad

My mother used to prepare a huge bowl of this salad every Christmas and we would feast on it for days as we ate our way through the rest of the turkey and ham. It tasted better and better as we got to the end! The dill-pickled cucumbers (we used Polski Ogorki brand) and capers add just enough of a tang to counteract the smooth blandness of the potatoes. The dressing can be made in a food processor or with a rotary mixer.

2 kg potatoes (about 8 large potatoes)
8 eggs, hard-boiled
500 g jar dill-pickled cucumbers, drained

¼ cup capers, drained
¼ cup chopped fresh dill

DRESSING
2 egg yolks
juice of a lemon
1 tsp mild French mustard

freshly ground black pepper
⅔ cup olive oil

Boil the potatoes unpeeled until just cooked but still firm. When cool enough to handle, slip the skins off, cut into small (1-cm) dice and place in a large mixing bowl.

Shell the eggs and chop finely. Slice the drained cucumbers lengthwise and then into 1-cm pieces. If capers are large, slice in half.

Add the egg, dill-pickled cucumbers and capers to the bowl. Spoon dressing over, add dill and mix with a large spoon to combine. Cover and refrigerate until needed. Can be made three or four days ahead and stored in the refrigerator for up to 10 days.

To make the dressing, place the yolks in the bowl of the processor with lemon juice, mustard and pepper. With processor running, pour a thin stream of oil into the processor, a little at a time, until the mixture thickens. Gradually add as much of the oil as is needed to make a stiff mixture. Do not over mix.

Serves 15–20

Bigos

Polish Hunters' Stew

୧⊙(⊙)ᒣ

It's been said that there are as many versions of Poland's famed bigos as there are cooks in Poland! Here I present the version my mother taught me, which was no doubt adapted slightly to our Australian climate and ingredients. It is a hearty, warming dish, wonderful on cold nights in winter. Bigos is best made 2–3 days in advance and re-heated before serving.

2 tbsp butter
1 onion, chopped
2 rashers bacon, chopped (or 100 g ham pieces)
500 g diced lean pork
700 g can sauerkraut
100 g Polish salami, chopped

¼ fresh Savoy cabbage (around 500 g), finely shredded
1 large green cooking apple, peeled and chopped
about 6 cups water
½ tsp caraway seeds
freshly ground black pepper

Heat half the butter in a frying pan and gently fry the onion and bacon for 2–3 minutes until soft. Transfer the onion mixture to a large casserole or heavy-based saucepan. Add the remaining butter to the pan, heat and add half the diced pork. Sauté on all sides to just brown, then transfer to the casserole. Repeat with the remaining pork.

Drain the sauerkraut and rinse once with cold water to remove excess salt, if necessary. Add to the casserole along with the salami, apple and water. Add only enough water to make mixture sloppy but not too watery. As a guide, the level of the water should be three-quarters up the side of the sauerkraut mixture in the casserole.

At this stage, the dish looks more cabbage than meat. This is fine; the cabbage will soften and condense in size during cooking. Cover and simmer gently on low heat for 45 minutes. Add the caraway and pepper and continue to simmer for a further 45 minutes.

Serve with boiled potatoes and soft rye bread.

Serves 8–10

Anne's Sweet Cheese-filled Crepes

When Anne made crepes, we'd all line up. She made up this lovely cheese filling using a mix of farm cheese and a type of crème fraiche but you can use ricotta or mascarpone instead. It was a lot of fiddle but they were incredibly popular. Use your favourite pancake or crepe recipe to make the crepes. Anne's were very thin, so a recipe like Gabriel Gaté's on page 45 would be perfect.

500 g farm cheese or full-fat thick ricotta
250 g sour cream or crème fraiche or mascarpone
4 egg yolks
¾ cup (100 g) currants

2 lemons
2 oranges
⅓ cup (75 g) caster sugar
pure vanilla essence
12–16 prepared crepes
butter, for frying

Place the farm cheese, sour cream, egg yolks and currants in a large mixing bowl.

Zest the lemons and oranges and add to the bowl along with the sugar and vanilla. Combine all ingredients well with a large spoon. You can cover and refrigerate the filling now overnight or until you're ready to fill the crepes.

When ready to serve, place 3–4 tablespoons of the cheese mixture on top of each crepe and roll up. Continue until all the filling is used up.

Heat the butter in a frypan, add the filled and rolled crepes to the pan without overcrowding them and pan-fry until just golden and heated through. Turn once or twice to brown evenly. You're simply heating the filling and crisping the outside so don't overcook or the crepes will become tough. Serve with a fork and knife.

Makes enough filling for 12–16 crepes

Feasts and festivals

Christmas was always huge. We would celebrate with a meatless
dinner on Christmas Eve, as is traditional in Europe, but with every
type of fish and seafood you could imagine. It was a real fusion
between superb Australian produce and old-world Polish customs.
No one would dare start eating until we had each exchanged a kiss
and swapped a sliver of *oplatek*, thin white Communion wafer that
my family would post from Poland each and every Christmas. Then
we'd tuck in to our heart's content.

Similarly Easter was pretty big too. As a child, I loved peeling
Anne's brown hard-boiled eggs which were coloured by boiling
the eggs in a large pot of water with brown onion skins.

Steven Snow and his mother, Jean Sheedy

Having a mother and grandmother who had lived in Pakistan before migrating to Australia meant I enjoyed exotic foods from a young age. While the other kids were 'enjoying' Devon and tomato sandwiches at school, I loved last night's curry between two pieces of bread.

The cauliflower and broccoli bake was brilliant and instilled a love of vegetables. My friends found it a welcome respite from the water-logged mushy insipid offerings they were used to. The tuna casserole was my first introduction to fish and spice and I am still hooked. As for banana loaf—it is still my coffee accompaniment of choice. Writing this brief little introduction has really clarified why I eat and cook as I do. Thanks Mum.

Cauliflower and Broccoli Bake

✑◗◐◗✎

This vegetable bake of Mum's served 4–6 people if you did not allow teenagers to be part of the mix.

125 g shell pasta, cooked al
    dente and drained
½ small cauliflower, cut into
    florets
250 g broccoli, cut into florets
2 rashers bacon, chopped
1 onion, chopped
a little extra virgin olive oil

30 g butter or margarine
2 tbsp plain flour
1½ cups milk
½ cup cream
salt and freshly ground pepper
1 cup fresh breadcrumbs
60 g grated cheese

Preheat the oven to 180°C.

Spoon the pasta into a lightly greased ovenproof dish. Cook the cauliflower and broccoli in the microwave until just tender. Sauté the bacon and onion in a small frying pan in a little olive oil then combine the vegetables and the onion and bacon mixture with the pasta.

To make the roux, melt the butter in a small saucepan and stir in the flour. Gradually add the milk and cream, stirring constantly over medium heat until the sauce boils. Season to taste with a little salt and pepper.

Pour the sauce over the pasta and vegetables and stir to mix well. Sprinkle the top with the fresh breadcrumbs and cheese and bake for 30–40 minutes.

Serves 4

Tuna Casserole

✑◗◐◗✎

I use Bolst's curry powder mixed with a little vinegar to make a curry paste for this recipe. To make 3 cups cooked rice you need 1 cup uncooked rice. A medium-grain rice is best for this dish.

1 onion, diced finely
vegetable oil
1 tbsp curry paste or powder, or
   to taste
425 g can tomatoes

2–3 cups cooked rice
1 large can (425 g) tuna in
   spring water
1 cup fresh breadcrumbs
60 g grated cheese

Preheat the oven to 180°C. Lightly grease an ovenproof dish.

Sauté the onion in a frying pan in a little oil until it is lightly browned. Add the curry paste, stirring until fragrant, then mix in the tomatoes. Cook gently for 10–15 minutes. Add the rice and stir well.

Drain the tuna and break into small pieces, reserving the liquid. Spoon a layer of the rice mixture over the bottom of the ovenproof dish and top with a layer of tuna. Repeat alternate layering and finish with a layer of breadcrumbs and grated cheese on top. Pour over the reserved liquid from the tuna can and bake for 30 minutes until the cheese and breadcrumbs are golden brown. Serve with salad.

Serves 4

Banana Loaf

You need ripe to slightly over-ripe bananas for this fruit loaf. If you use self-raising flour, it takes less time to cook.

120 g butter
1 cup caster sugar
2 eggs
2 large bananas, mashed
2 cups plain flour

1 tsp bi-carb soda
½ tsp salt
¼ cup milk
1 tsp lemon juice
½ cup chopped nuts

Preheat the oven to 180°C. Grease a 22-cm loaf pan.

Beat the butter, sugar, eggs and bananas together in a bowl. Stir in the flour, bi-carb soda, salt, milk, lemon juice and nuts. Spoon the batter into the loaf pan and bake for 45–55 minutes or until it springs back when lightly touched. Leave for a few minutes to cool before turning out onto a wire rack.

Kathy Snowball and her mother, Shirley McAllister

I grew up in a family of women. My poor father was totally outnumbered. There was Mum, me and my sister, my grandmother and my great grandmother all living under the one roof. My great grandmother had lived in the outback and cooked on sheep stations for the shearers, so there was a tradition in our household of big meals, cooked plainly, with the emphasis on meat. We all loved our food, but there wasn't much variety.

You could tell what day of the week it was by what Mum served—steak on Monday, chops on Tuesday, fish on Friday, roast lamb on Sunday and so on. The ingredients were always good, but Mum was never guilty of undercooking anything.

One of our treats from a very early age was to have fresh bottled oysters, brought back from a weekend excursion to the Hawkesbury River. They were very exotic and we often had them topped with grilled bacon and Worcestershire sauce.

She also made a great roast. Mum made mint sauce whenever she cooked any lamb dish, with mint from the garden. Along with parsley they were the only herbs we grew. She also made excellent biscuits, like the recipe here. They are simple, so we were able to help rolling them out.

I loved to help in the kitchen and would beg Mum to bake, particularly on wet Sunday afternoons, so we could then sit around and devour our efforts. Mum's specialties were boiled fruit cake and something we called 'pufftaloonies', fried pumpkin scones. Sadly I don't have the recipe for these!

Mum had polio as a small child and had lost much of the use of her right arm, however this didn't hold her back and in fact I think it made her even more determined. She could drive a car and was very able in the kitchen. She peeled, chopped, stuffed and rolled along with the best and entertained regularly, especially Saturday night supper and cards. Her specialities were grilled prunes in bacon and lemon cheesecake.

Mum was a good plain cook, never a great cook, but was always very generous and hospitable and she instilled in me the importance of good food and that family life revolved around the kitchen.

Boned Rolled Shoulder of Lamb with Mint Sauce

We all got to choose dinner for our birthday and boned shoulder of lamb was my favourite. Mum used malt vinegar to make mint sauce because that was what was available, but you could use white wine vinegar or cider vinegar. She always served plenty of roast potatoes, pumpkin and sweet potato with roast lamb, and peas, always peas. Whenever I cook roast lamb, I think of my mum.

MINT SAUCE
2 tbsp finely chopped mint
1 tsp sugar

1 tbsp boiling water
¼ cup malt vinegar

STUFFING
2 cups soft breadcrumbs
1 onion, finely chopped
¼ cup finely chopped herbs,
   including parsley and mint

2 rashers bacon, finely chopped
1 egg
grated rind of a lemon

900 g boned shoulder of lamb
1 tbsp olive oil

1 tbsp plain flour

Preheat the oven to 200°C.

For the mint sauce, combine the mint, sugar and water, then stir in the vinegar.

For the stuffing, combine the breadcrumbs with the remaining ingredients and season to taste.

Lay the lamb flat on the bench and place the stuffing along one side. Roll up to enclose the filling and tie with string. Rub the lamb with the oil and season with salt and pepper. Place the lamb in a roasting pan along with enough water so that it comes up to about 1 cm and roast, uncovered, for 1 hour. Remove the lamb from pan and rest, loosely covered with foil in a warm place for 10 minutes.

To make the gravy, add the flour to the pan juices and stir over medium heat for 1 minute. Add a little water, season to taste and stir to form a thin gravy.

Serve the lamb sliced, with gravy and mint sauce.

Serves 4

Mrs Heath's Jam Biscuits

I don't know who Mrs Heath was, and Mum never said, but as children we loved helping to make these biscuits and sandwiching them with jam. They are best eaten within a few days of baking, otherwise they go a bit soggy, which is how we used to like them.

250 g soft butter
½ cup firmly packed brown
   sugar
1 cup caster sugar
2 eggs

2¾ cups plain flour
1 tsp bicarbonate of soda
½ tsp ground cinnamon
⅓ cup strawberry jam

Preheat the oven to 180°C. Line 2 oven trays with baking paper.

Beat the butter and both sugars with electric mixer until light and fluffy. Add the eggs one at a time, beating to combine. Stir in the sifted flour combined with the bicarbonate of soda and cinnamon. Cover and refrigerate 30 minutes.

Roll level tablespoons of the mixture into balls. Place on the lined oven trays, about 8 cm apart and flatten with the heel of your hand and bake for 12 minutes.

When biscuits are cool enough to handle, sandwich them together with a little jam.

Makes about 25

Charmaine Solomon and her mother, Kitty Perera

Deborah Solomon and her mother, Charmaine Solomon

Jenna Hand and her mother, Deborah Solomon

Cookery writer Charmaine Solomon has been making her presence felt in our kitchens and in kitchens around the world for over 40 years. Uniquely in this book, the stories that follow cover four generations of one family with recipes their mothers loved to cook, making mealtimes and after-school-times not only a delicious but memorable tradition.

Charmaine

Mum's recipes! Who am I kidding? Mum didn't use recipes. She cooked superb food, but it was all done by instinct. A little of this and a lot of that. Measurements? Never.

When I praised a dish she made and requested it again, it was nothing like the one I remembered from a couple of days before. Good, but quite different.

Perhaps it is this sort of experience which led me into my career, determined that my recipes would be accurate and anyone using them would get the results they were expecting, every time.

Crab Curry

While Mum didn't win every battle with the huge mud crabs she would buy (live and bent on escape), she managed to subdue them despite the odd pinch by their claws. She was fearless, and dispatched them with a large kitchen knife in double quick time. They would be cooked before they realised they were dead!

2 large mud crabs, females if
    possible
3 medium onions, finely
    chopped
6 cloves garlic, finely chopped
2 tsp finely grated fresh ginger
½ tsp fenugreek seeds
3 sprigs fresh curry leaves
1 small stick cinnamon

2 tsp chilli powder
1 tsp ground turmeric
3 tsp salt
4 cups thin coconut milk
    (see tip)
2 tbsp desiccated coconut
1 tbsp ground rice
2 cups thick coconut milk
3 tbsp lemon juice

To clean the crabs, remove the large carapace and discard the fibrous tissue found under the shell (pointed white things known as 'dead men's fingers'). Divide each crab into 4 portions, cutting each body in halves and separating the large claws from the body. Leave the legs attached to body.

Put the onion, garlic, ginger, fenugreek seeds, curry leaves, cinnamon stick, chilli, turmeric, salt and thin coconut milk mixture into a large saucepan. Cover and simmer gently 30 minutes. Add the crabs and cook for 20 minutes. If the pan is not large enough, simmer half the pieces of crab at a time. The crab should be submerged in the sauce while it cooks.

Heat the desiccated coconut and ground rice separately in a dry frying pan over medium heat, stirring constantly to prevent burning, until both are golden brown. Put both in an electric blender, add 1 cup of the thick coconut milk, cover and blend on high speed for 1 minute. Add to the curry with the lemon juice. 'Wash out' the blender with the remaining coconut milk and add to the curry, too. Simmer uncovered for a further 10 minutes. Serve with boiled rice.

Tip: to make 4 cups thin coconut milk, combine 1 × 400 ml can coconut milk with water in a measuring jug to make 1 litre.

Serves 4

Fresh Cream Fudge

My mum had the sweetest tooth. Her cakes and desserts were legendary, if unpredictable. Despite suffering from adult onset diabetes, she would cook up a pan of fudge from time to time, and tell me it was for visitors. While she didn't cut herself squares of this candy, she would scrape the pan. My daughter Nina has taken over as the 'Fudge Queen', and here is her recipe.

400 g can sweetened condensed
   milk
½ cup cream

1½ cups sugar
60 g butter
2 tsp vanilla

Combine all ingredients except vanilla in a large heavy saucepan, preferably one that is non-stick. Stir over medium heat until it reaches the soft ball stage (a little dropped into a cup of iced water should form a soft ball immediately). Remove pan from heat at once and stand in a larger pan of cold water for a few minutes to cool slightly. Add the vanilla and beat until the fudge thickens and starts to lose its gloss. Immediately stop beating and pour into a buttered 20-cm square cake pan. Mark into squares and cut when cold, using a sawing motion.

Makes about 25 4-cm pieces

Avocado Fool

Amazingly enough, coming from a tropical country where avocados were plentiful, I had never encountered an avocado salad or sandwich. It was always a sweet—quickly made and smooth and rich, it hardly needs a recipe. Simply scoop fully ripe but not overripe avocado out of its skin and mash until smooth with caster sugar and cream. Or, to be more authentically tropical, sweetened condensed milk—a more realistic option in a country where dairy products like fresh cream were not readily available.

Deborah

All my life I have been lucky to be surrounded by women who loved to cook and eat. My grandmother came to Australia when I was only three, but I still remember her doing a cook-off in the garage of *balauchaung*—the delicious, pungent prawn relish from Burma, the land of her birth. She could also take down a banana tree with a Chinese cleaver to make *mohinga* and dismember a live crab with no need to resort to the kind of mental gymnastics I do to overcome my squeamishness.

My relationship with my grandmother started in earnest when she eventually came to Australia, some 11 years after she promised to arrive. The life of the party, a real 'Merry Widow', she was more often guest than host, but she definitely knew her way around the spice cupboard and could create delicious dishes from next to no ingredients. Her New Year's Day feasts quickly became a family tradition.

With my mother being the Asian cooking legend, Charmaine Solomon, my first instinct was to choose recipes reflecting that culinary background. However, it is the simple crepe that is one of my earliest food memories. As the children of two working parents, knowing Mum had started her holidays made us all run the last block of the long trip from school to devour those crepes hot with lemon and sugar as a rare afternoon treat.

Chicken Kiev

Long before there were chicken shops which sell such things mass produced, Mum spent many hours perfecting Chicken Kiev. I can still see the garlicky butter spurting out of the golden crumbed chicken as the fork pierced it. Heaven.

In days of old this was made with the half chicken breast leaving the wing bone intact. I can see that plays no practical purpose unless you want to go very retro and outfit it with a white paper frill. I recommend using free-range chicken.

75 g unsalted butter, softened
¼ tsp crushed fresh garlic
½ tsp salt
1 tsp finely chopped parsley
1 tsp lemon juice

2 single chicken breasts
plain flour, for dipping
1 egg, beaten
breadcrumbs
oil, for deep frying

Combine the softened butter with the garlic, salt, parsley and lemon juice. Place on a sheet of cling wrap, fold the cling wrap over and form the butter into a neat rectangle. Freeze the butter while preparing the chicken.

Place each single chicken breast on a sheet of freezer wrap and cover with another piece. Use a rolling pin, bottle or the side of a meat mallet to flatten the chicken gently, being very careful not to break the flesh. Aim for about 1 cm thickness.

Unwrap the butter, cut into two sticks, and place one on each chicken breast. Roll up folding in the sides to form a neat cylinder, being careful to fully enclose the butter.

Dip each piece of chicken in flour, beaten egg and finally breadcrumbs. Place on a clean plate and refrigerate for at least 1 hour to set the coating, so that it sticks to the chicken when you cook it.

Heat the oil in a small, deep pan or wok. Get the oil just hot enough to brown a small square (crouton) of bread in 1 minute—any hotter and the outside of the chicken will brown before the inside is cooked. Cook the chicken breasts for 4–5 minutes. If they are cooking too quickly, lower the heat. Drain on absorbent paper and serve immediately with steamed seasonal vegetables.

Serves 2

Crepes

This basic crepe batter was from my mother's Best of Belle *cookbook, a collection of recipes from the time she was food editor for that magazine in the early 1980s. I have modified it slightly (sorry Mum) and used light milk instead of equal parts of milk and water. Either way, they are fabulous. If you like them thicker, slightly reduce the quantity of milk. They can be eaten simply with sugar and fresh lemon juice as we did as an after-school snack or used as the basis of a savoury dish.*

4 eggs
2 cups light (low-fat) milk
½ tsp salt

1 cup plain flour
1 tbsp melted butter
extra butter, to grease pan

Place the eggs and milk in a large jug and blend with a stick blender. Add the salt, flour and melted butter and blend again. Strain into a fresh jug if you think there may be any lumps in it. Let the mixture stand in the fridge for 1 hour.

Heat a crepe pan and grease with butter. Pour in a ¼ cup or so of the batter and swirl it around to cover the base of the crepe pan evenly. Quickly pour any excess batter back into the jug. Cook over high heat until the top of the crepe looks moist rather than wet. The bottom should be golden. Quickly flip the crepe and let the other side cook for about 30 seconds. Stack on a plate and repeat the process until all the batter is used.

Makes about 18 crepes

Rose and Lychee Ice-cream

Mum adored the roses in a neighbouring street so Dad planted 25 rose bushes in our garden for her. The scent of those old-fashioned crimson blossoms was the inspiration for many jars of rose-petal conserve. Where roses are concerned scent trumps shape, and home-grown, unsprayed blooms are the only choice for cooking.

I remember making ice-cream on hot summer evenings. The entire family would take turns—literally—with the hand-cranked salt and ice churn. When eventually it was so frozen that even Dad couldn't budge it we would stand by, ready for a helping of this marvellous frozen treat.

My mother gave me a superb electric refrigerated ice-cream maker for my thirtieth birthday. It has churned its way through many delightful desserts since then. While lychee and rose was not a flavour combination she handed down to me, their flavours marry beautifully and pay tribute to the fragrant blossoms that grew in my parents' little garden of Eden. When in season we use longans, a fruit similar to lychee, which now grow in place of the roses.

ROSE AND LYCHEE INFUSION
1 cup canned or fresh lychees
250 ml lychee juice or syrup
   from the can

⅓ cup sugar
2 large, fragrant, unsprayed Mr
   Lincoln roses

CUSTARD
300 ml cream
6 egg yolks
¼ cup sugar

3 drops red food colour
1 tbsp rose water, if necessary

To make the infusion, chop the lychees into small pieces and set aside. Heat the lychee juice or syrup and when boiling add the sugar, stirring to dissolve. Remove from heat and add the petals of both the roses. When cool, strain and finely chop a tablespoon of the petals to stir through the custard.

While heating the cream to scalding point to make the custard, whisk the yolks and the sugar until light in colour. Add the hot cream gradually to the yolks then pour the mixture back into the pan and cook over low heat, stirring constantly until the custard thickens. Remove from the heat and add the strained lychee syrup.

Refrigerate until cold then stir through the chopped lychees and rose petals. Taste and add extra rose essence as necessary and only enough red colouring to turn the mixture a pretty pale pink.

Churn according to instructions of your ice-cream churn if you have one, or pour into a bowl and freeze until slushy. Remove from freezer, beat and return to freeze again. Repeat and then let freeze fully. Put the ice-cream in the refrigerator to soften slightly just before serving.

Makes 6 generous serves

Jenna

We ate extraordinarily well at home. My mother, a professional cook, and my cookbook-author grandmother made everything from scratch. I assumed this was normal until the afternoon a school friend came over for home-made pikelets. I can still remember her approving words as she reached for a second: 'These are really yummy. What packet did they come out of?' My sister and I were horrified.

Mum had trained her daughters well. As children, our revulsion at eating anything that had to be reconstituted or scooped out of a can was extreme, and she took full advantage of it. Some kids feared the wooden spoon, others the belt strap. For my sister and I, nothing struck terror in our hearts more than Mum standing in the hallway brandishing a tin of spaghetti and meatballs. 'Stop pinching your sister or you'll get *this* for dinner! Cold!'

These days Mum encourages my own culinary experiments and is always generous with her advice. Sometimes too generous. My dad has reached the stage where he bans Mum from the kitchen while he's cooking. He'd rather do it the wrong way but his way, than be corrected on knife selection or ingredient substitution as if he is working in a Michelin-starred establishment.

To be fair, she is often justified. On one memorable occasion, Dad made dinner for us kids while Mum was out. The fish looked nice enough but it tasted pretty awful. When we told him, Dad was full of indignation. He insisted he had followed Mum's instructions and had even picked fresh spring onions from the garden. The meals went in the bin. We went to our rooms. Mum came home, looked at the green stuff in the kitchen and wondered aloud what her daffodils were doing on the chopping board. Vindicated.

Vegetarian Chilli Bean Stew

Mum gave me this recipe when I left home and moved into a student share house. It's tasty, simple and you can buy the ingredients out of the spare change from your textbooks. This chilli can be served with corn tortillas or taco shells along with grated tasty cheese, shredded lettuce and sliced avocado.

2 onions, chopped
2 tbsp olive oil
5 cloves garlic, finely chopped
1 red chilli, seeded and chopped
1 cup corn kernels, frozen will
   do nicely
1 red or yellow capsicum,
   seeded and chopped
2 tsp Mexican chilli powder

2 tsp ground cumin
2 tsp ground coriander
750 ml bottle tomato passata (or
   tomato puree)
½ cup burghul (cracked wheat)
2 × 440 g cans red kidney
   beans, drained and rinsed
2 × 440 g cans chickpeas,
   drained and rinsed

Sauté the onions in oil in a medium to large saucepan. When tender, add the garlic, chilli, corn kernels and capsicum and stir for a minute or two longer. Add spices and cook a further minute then add the tomato passata and the burghul and simmer for 15 minutes.

If you are feeding a crowd—8 people—add all four cans of beans and cook a further 15 minutes. If not, you can reserve half of what you have cooked. Place it in a freezer container then label and date it. Anytime in the next 6 months, you can defrost it, adding 1 can of red kidney beans and 1 can of chickpeas when heating.

Serves 4–8

Upside-down Peach Pancake

A Sunday breakfast treat for when stone fruit is at its peak. You can use nectarines instead of peaches.

6 eggs
50 g sugar
30 ml brandy or apple juice
100 g plain flour

8 peaches, sliced into eighths
150 g raw sugar
3 tbsp oil

Preheat the oven to 220°C.

Separate the eggs. Add sugar and brandy to the yolks and beat, then add the flour to thicken. Whisk the egg whites until stiff and fold into the yolk mixture.

Heat a heavy ovenproof 28-cm frying pan on the stove to very hot and add the peach slices. Add the raw sugar and oil and toss until a golden-brown caramel forms. Pour the pancake mixture over the peaches and place the pan in the hot oven for 5–10 minutes. To serve, place a large serving plate face down over the pancake in the pan then quickly invert.

Serves 4–6

Molten Chocolate Puddings

These impressive little desserts are surprisingly easy to make. Just don't tell the dinner guests.

125 g unsalted butter
125 g dark chocolate
2 vanilla beans or 1 tsp vanilla
   extract

2 tbsp brandy (optional)
4 eggs
150 g caster sugar
50 g plain flour

Preheat oven to 200°C. Grease the insides of 4 × 250-ml ramekins, or 6 slightly smaller ones, with butter and dust with sugar. Refrigerate until needed.

Melt the butter, chocolate and vanilla (and brandy if using) in a glass bowl over simmering water. Beat the sugar and eggs until foamy and the sugar has dissolved. Drizzle in the melted chocolate mixture. Sift in the flour and beat slowly to combine.

Pour into the prepared moulds, place them all on a tray and bake for 10 minutes (or 12 for the larger ones). Turn out onto individual plates by placing a plate on top of the ramekin and then flipping the whole thing over. Gently raise the ramekin up to remove. Serve with berries and vanilla ice-cream.

Serves 4–6

Craig Squire and his mother, Pamela Blakeway

Like most Anglo-Aussie families of the 1960s and 1970s, the meals at home were simple. For us, dinner was at lunch-time and tea was dinner, served early, so in summer with daylight saving it felt we were eating in the middle of the day and then into bed while it was still light. We always sat at the table, which was set properly, we spoke when spoken to, and heard stories of when times were tough. I had to hide the Brussels sprouts and flush them down the toilet, because we had to finish everything on the plate. We had a simple start—I can remember a meat safe at home, and the ice truck along with the butcher and greengrocer making home deliveries.

Dad's favourite meal was lamb's fry and bread with dripping and Mum and Dad's special treat was a glass of hock and a glass of beer. My brother had jam and cream on white bread every night after 'tea', and he still does!

Savoury Steak

This recipe was a winter staple; I think we had it with mash. It comes from the 1st Glenroy Scouts' Cookbook *circa 1971. This dish could be improved with a little red wine, some thyme, and even crisp bacon stirred through at the end. I have just changed the measures to metric.*

450 g gravy beef
1 tbsp plain flour
pinch nutmeg
salt and pepper
1 tbsp each tomato and
    Worcestershire sauce

1 tbsp vinegar
1 tsp sugar
½ pint (300 ml) water

Cut gravy beef into cubes. Mix flour with nutmeg, salt and pepper.

Roll beef cubes in seasoned flour.

Mix sauces, vinegar, sugar in water.

Place meat in casserole dish and pour liquid over.

Cover and cook in a moderate (180°C) oven for 2 hours.

Serves 4

Yoghurt Slice

When Mum was being a fitness fanatic, the food at home changed for the better; it became fresher and tastier. Salads and barbecues became more regular, and we had fewer slow-cooked oven dishes. I think I could tell that I would never have to eat another white lamb stew again, thank God. I hated yoghurt slice at first, but I had it so often it grew on me. I even had to have it at school, and now I think back to it with fondness. I have this recipe written out in Mum's writing, although it originally came from the Australian Weight Watchers Manual. *Mum noted that you can vary the dried fruit, add almonds on top, or serve hot or cold with stewed fruits.*

200 g natural yoghurt
½ cup plain cottage cheese
2 eggs, beaten
3 tbsp sultanas
3 tbsp wholemeal flour

1 tbsp wheatgerm or
   unprocessed bran
1 tbsp artificial sweetener
   (I would use raw sugar)
pinch cinnamon and nutmeg
½ tsp vanilla essence

Preheat the oven to 190°C. Lightly grease a narrow cake pan (25 × 7.5 cm).

Mix all ingredients well. Pour mix into cake pan and sprinkle extra nutmeg on top. Bake for 40 minutes. Cool and then refrigerate.

Serves 12

Trying new things

In the 1970s Mum and Dad went to and hosted dinner parties, they were pretty trendy! I think the pressure would have been on for Mum to be creative and the Scout recipe book would have had a work out. We had some "foreign" friends and they cooked really different food, and it tasted great. I had an Italian mate in high school, and mealtimes were very different at Ben's. They were loud and raucous and we all passed things around and wiped our mouths on the tablecloth. There was always something on the stove and mess in the kitchen was OK.

When I started my apprenticeship, I had never seen a zucchini or continental cucumber—I was very embarrassed when I didn't know which one to get from the coolroom. I had to learn pretty much from scratch, but I learnt fast.

Mum taught me how to work hard, respect my elders and listen. The rest came easy.

Ryan Squires and his mother, Janice Squires

Fresh pasta would have to be one of the most memorable things my mother cooked. Now I know why—quick, easy, large yield, versatile and low cost. Not that we had a big family (except when the Italian rellies from North Queensland visited). My mother also used to dry the fresh pasta out and keep it for another time.

Mum's family came over from Italy in the late 1920s. They settled in North Queensland and introduced new tobacco growing techniques and varieties. They later grew peanuts, sugar cane, sorghum and watermelons. She let me know how hard it was back then. This may have made me more appreciative of simple, traditional, Italian peasant food: bitter chicory, white crusty bread, home-made vinegar, Parma ham, salami and freshly made pasta.

All my mother's friends tell me how lucky I am to have a mother who cooks like Janice. Mum was even the pastry chef of one of Brisbane's best restaurants in the 1970s and early 1980s called Rags, in Caxton Street. Mum says that her nonna, Elisabeta Scarabello, had the most influence on her cooking.

Fresh Pasta with Fried Baby Onions and Parmigiano Reggiano

Sweet onions are best for this recipe, which reminds me of my mum's but actually was inspired by a restaurant in California's Napa Valley.

250 g plain flour
5 egg yolks
1 whole egg
splash milk
splash extra virgin olive oil
4 baby onions, sliced 3 mm thick
olive oil and canola oil, for
  frying

salt and pepper
unsalted butter
sea salt
a few drops vinegar
a little parmigiano reggiano,
  shaved

Reserving half a handful of flour (so you can adjust the texture of the dough), pour the remaining flour onto a wooden pasta board and shape into a mound. Make a well in the centre and add the egg yolks, whole egg and splashes of oil and milk. Slowly, starting in the centre and working outwards, mix the dough until combined. Use the reserved flour to adjust the texture—it should be non-sticky to the touch. Knead to a smooth, elastic and soft texture (this should take 10 minutes of good hard kneading). Wrap in plastic wrap and rest in the refrigerator for at least 30 minutes.

Place the sliced onions in a saucepan and cover with enough oil to fry (about 1 tbsp olive oil to 3 tbsp canola). Slowly bring the oil to a high heat and fry the onions until they are golden brown, sweet and chewy. Drain well and season. Keep warm.

Cut the dough into 4 pieces. Roll the first piece through your pasta machine set at thickest level a couple of times, then roll it through on each setting working to the finest. Repeat with the remaining pieces of dough. At this point, you can either replace the attachment with a self cutter or use a knife to cut the pasta into 1-cm wide strips that are as long as possible. Feel free to cut thinner strips if you want.

Cook the fresh pasta in a large saucepan of simmering water. It will only take a minute or two. Drain, tip the pasta back into the warm pot, add a knob or two of butter, some sea salt and a few drops of vinegar (it balances the flavour). Top with the fried onions and shaved reggiano.

Serves 4

Deep Fried Red-beak Gar

I also remember times when Grandpa and I headed to the coast for a 'drag of the net' to catch 'red-beak gar' (eastern sea garfish). If we had no luck, he would swap some 'chop chop' (fresh tobacco) with his mate—or maybe it was another family member—for the freshest reef fish money couldn't buy. Mum and her mother would do the rest, but not without asking every member of the family, 'How do you like it done?' This fish would be a nice addition to the bitter chicory and the 38-year-old fermented red wine. Select red-beak no bigger than 13 cm long, the smaller the better for this recipe, so you can eat it whole.

whole red-beak gar
plain flour, for dusting
2 litres peanut oil

sea salt
vinegar or juice of a lemon

Scale and gut the red-beak and pat dry. Dust lightly with flour, shaking off any excess.

Heat the oil to a sizzle (roughly 180°C) in a large saucepan. Place the fish in the hot oil. Don't overcrowd the pan. For the best result cook them 2 or 3 at a time. When they are golden brown and the fins are crispy, carefully lift them out, drain on absorbent paper towel and while hot, season with salt. Keep warm and repeat the process until all the fish are cooked. Douse with vinegar or lemon juice and sprinkle with your favourite herb. Eat whole straight away.

Crostoli

This crostoli recipe is straight from my mother's aunt, Tuila Piagno.

3 eggs
1½ tbsp caster sugar
1 tsp water
30 ml brandy
finely grated orange rind

3 cups plain flour
lard and peanut oil, for frying
white sugar or icing sugar, for
   dusting

Beat the eggs and sugar with the water and brandy. Add the orange rind. Add the flour and knead well to a smooth dough. Divide the dough into quarters and dust well with a little extra flour.

Using a pasta machine, pass one piece of dough through the largest setting 3 times, then roll it through on each setting, gradually reaching the finest setting. Cut the sheets of dough with a ravioli roller cutter into 10 cm × 4 cm rectangles, making a small slit down the centre of each.

Heat equal parts lard and peanut oil together to very hot (roughly 180°C) and fry the pieces of dough in batches. Lift out as soon as they are done (they'll have uniform air bubbles all over), drain and dust with sugar while hot. Eat right now or store when cooled in an airtight container.

Makes 60

Tony Tan and his mother, Lim Kiem Keow

When the people from the tropical isle of Hainan, off China's southern coast, left their native villages, little did they realise they would place their indelible culinary mark on South-East Asia. Known as the Hainanese, this Chinese dialect-group speak a divergent Min dialect which is associated to the Fujianes. They are credited for bringing two culinary traditions to Singapore and Malaysia—coffee shops and Hainanese Chicken Rice.

This renowned chicken rice is directly linked to the great diaspora of the Hainanese in the late nineteenth and the twentieth centuries. A three-in-one meal, it is a classic composition of poached chicken, rice and soup. Deceptively simple to prepare, yet often misinterpreted, the chicken requires nothing more than precise timing to achieve perfect succulence and a melting quality.

Teamed with rice cooked with the poaching stock and some chilli sauce, it is a dish without peer. It is also synonymous with the way I think what food ought to be—unfussy, simple and cooked with love and care.

It is a dish much relished in my family during festivals or whenever there is a celebration, or whenever we felt like it. I cannot precisely remember the moment when I first ate chicken rice. I do, however, recollect scenes of my parents and relatives preparing it as a sort of family ritual. As only the best ingredients were used, capons were preferred then. The responsibility of despatching and cleaning the prized chooks invariably fell into the hands to my brother-in-law.

My mother and relatives picked through a mountain of red chillies for the sauce.

My sister and I usually picked, cleaned and rinsed the rice. I also have fond memories of the sweet, aromatic odours of the rice drifting from the kitchen through the house as much as I remember the morsels of choice, luscious meat over the bowls of heavenly rice.

Hundreds of recipes and thousands of interpretations exist for this classic dish. Some people insist on two separate sauces, one of ginger and the other chilli, instead of the combined sauce. Others prefer bean shoots in the soup. We do agree on one point though: Hainanese chicken rice at its source is never served with chilli sauce—that is an innovation from Malaysia and Singapore.

My Mother's Hainanese Chicken Rice

In the time-honoured tradition, this recipe has been handed down from my mother and her mother before her.

1.8 kg free-range chicken
3 tsp salt
4 litres water
15 g ginger, about the size of a walnut, bashed with the side of your knife

1 bunch watercress from Asian grocers, picked
1 small cucumber, sliced
light soy sauce
sesame oil
coriander sprigs

CHILLI SAUCE
6 large red chillies, chopped
20 g ginger, sliced
4 cloves garlic

salt
juice of 2 limes

RICE
reserved chicken fat or 2 tbsp cooking oil
5 shallots, sliced
3 cloves garlic, minced

3 cups rice, washed and drained in a colander
2 pandan leaves, tied into a knot
chicken stock

Remove the pads of chicken fat from the cavity and set aside. Rub chicken inside and out with 1 teaspoon salt. Make a loop by slipping a cotton twine between the wings and breast, then set aside for 30 minutes—not chilled.

Meanwhile, make the chilli sauce by combining all the ingredients in a pestle or mortar or a food processor, making sure it is still slightly granular, not too fine.

To cook the chicken, bring the water, ginger and the rest of the salt to the boil in a large stock pot. Using the string, lift the chicken into the boiling water. Submerge for 30–60 seconds, then lift the chicken out, draining the water from the cavity. Repeat this process a couple of times. This is to make sure the water in the bird is hot enough for even cooking. Adjust the heat and cook in the slowly boiling water for 8 minutes. Put the lid on, turn off the heat and steep the chicken for 40 minutes. Lift gently, making sure no skin is broken. Drain the stock from the cavity and then plunge into cold water to stop the cooking. Lift out, pat dry gently and set aside. Reserve the chicken stock.

To cook the rice, either render the chicken fat down and discard the solids or heat the vegetable oil in a wok. Add the shallots to fry until golden, then add the garlic to fry for another minute. Add the rinsed rice. Fry until the rice begins to pop slightly from the wok. Transfer to a rice cooker or saucepan. Add the pandan leaves and pour hot stock over the rice to about just below the first joint of your index finger. Cook using the absorption method.

In the meantime, make the soup by putting 2 litres of the reserved chicken stock into a saucepan. Bring to the boil and add the watercress. Adjust the seasoning.

To serve, cut up the chicken Chinese style and arrange over a plate of sliced cucumber. Add a dash of soy sauce mixed with a touch of sesame oil over the chicken. Garnish with coriander sprigs. Serve chicken with individual bowls of rice accompanied by the watercress broth and offer chilli dipping sauce on the side.

Serves 4–6 with two other dishes

Josh Thomas and his mother, Rebecca Thomas

I loved my mum's custard when I was a kid. I loved it because it was lumpy. I have gotten pretty pedantic about my custard these days, and can think of few things worse than a lumpy custard. A little while back I was at Mum's house and I pointed out her custard had curdled. I don't think anything has ever broken her heart harder. For this book I have put in my rhubarb and custard recipe. This is my favourite custard recipe and I make it a lot. Never for my mum though. Every time I go over to her place now I ask her to make me 'lumpy custard like I love it!' and she smiles and I smile—and then I wonder what the hell was wrong with me when I was 12.

Lamb Tagine

Mum loves this tagine. Well, she didn't say anything bad about it and I will take that as a compliment. You don't need to cook this in a tagine. You just need a heavy pan with a lid. If you are short on time you can cook it in a pressure cooker. The method is exactly the same but you only cook it for 30 minutes instead of 2 hours.

2 tbsp vegetable oil
1 kg lamb (shoulder, leg), cut into 2-cm cubes
1 onion, chopped
2 cloves garlic, chopped
1 tsp ground coriander
1 tsp ground cumin
1 tsp ground turmeric
¼ tsp ground ginger
¼ tsp cayenne pepper
1 tsp ground cinnamon
1 tbsp chopped fresh coriander (stalks/root or leaves)

zest and juice of 1 orange
1 cup chicken stock
1 tbsp almond meal
½ cup roasted, blanched almonds, coarsely chopped
100 g pitted dates
salt and freshly ground black pepper

TO SERVE
cous cous
plain yoghurt
2 tbsp chopped fresh coriander

In a tagine, heat half the oil and brown the lamb in batches on a medium heat. Set aside.

Heat the remaining oil and fry the onion and garlic until translucent, add the spices and the fresh coriander and toast for around 5 minutes then add the browned lamb, orange zest and juice, chicken stock, almond meal and whole almonds and mix together well.

Cover and cook on a low heat for around 2 hours (until the lamb is as tender as you like it). Remove the lid, add the dates, and cook for a further 15 minutes until the sauce has thickened. Season to taste.

Serve on a bed of couscous with a dollop of yoghurt and top with some chopped fresh coriander.

Serves 4–6

Stewed Rhubarb

juice of 1–2 lemons
big bunch of rhubarb chopped
   into 2–3 cm-ish pieces

3 strips lemon rind
3 heaped tbsp sugar

To cook the rhubarb, tip the juice of 1–2 lemons into a saucepan so
that it completely covers the base. Add the rhubarb, lemon rind and
sugar. Place the lid on the pot and quickly bring to the boil, let bubble
for around a minute then remove from the heat. Leave it to steam in pot
for a few minutes then whip it with a fork (don't mash).

Serves 4

Custard

This custard recipe has corn flour in it, which helps stabilise the custard while it cooks and reduces the chance of it curdling. It also helps it thicken faster, although it does add a slightly chalky texture. If you are really confident with custard then try it without the corn flour.

1 cup milk
1 cup thick cream
1 vanilla bean, split in half
   lengthways
4 egg yolks

1 tbsp corn flour
⅓ cup caster sugar
stewed rhubarb, made from
   1 big bunch (see recipe
   opposite)

To make the custard, combine the milk and cream in a saucepan with the split vanilla bean and heat until it is almost boiling, but *don't let it boil.* You need to heat the milk for around 15 minutes to really get the flavour going. If you use vanilla extract instead of vanilla bean, you will need about 1 teaspoon. Make sure you use true or 'natural' vanilla extract, not the imitation 'artificial vanilla essence'.

In a mixing bowl, whisk together the egg yolks, corn flour and sugar.

With a slotted spoon, lift the vanilla bean out of the hot milk. Now tip some (or all) of the hot milk into the bowl with the egg yolks and whisk constantly so you have a creamy smooth paste.

Pour the custard mix into the saucepan and cook over a low heat, stirring constantly until the custard thickens and coats the back of the spoon (around 15 minutes). Make sure you are constantly scraping the bottom and sides of the pan. Don't leave the custard, don't look at or think of anything other than the custard while you are cooking it. The second you do, it will curdle. If you think it is too hot take it off the heat immediately and whisk. If you curdle the custard you can put it through a strainer, which will make it better but it will still be a bit shit.

To serve, spoon the stewed rhubarb into a bowl and top with the custard. Yum!

Serves 4

Hadleigh Troy and his mother, Jill Troy

Although Mum says she taught me everything she knows when it comes to cooking, those who know and love her are in on the joke.

Mum has never been the best cook—perhaps for lack of wanting to try, maybe she masterminded my destiny to become a chef. Her plan was, perhaps, to want me to cook for her. But it hasn't necessarily worked out that way, as I love being cooked for and I am probably the last person in the world to judge Mum's cooking! I am happy to receive a meal from Mum on the table, although this has become increasingly rare over the past few years with my busy schedule rarely allowing time for dinner at Mum's place …

Spaghetti Bolognese

My favourite meal to this day remains my childhood staple—Spaghetti Bolognese. I insist on this as often as possible for our family meal (aka staff meal) at the restaurant. It has since become a test of skills for every new member of the kitchen team for the very first meal that they prepare for the rest of the hungry team! The finished result always shows the love they have for cooking.

¼ cup olive oil
1 large onion, finely chopped
2 cloves garlic, crushed
2 rashers bacon, diced
500 g minced topside beef
425 g can peeled tomatoes, chopped
2 tbsp tomato paste
1 tbsp fresh oregano or 1 tsp dried oregano
½ tsp dried thyme
2 tbsp chopped fresh parsley
⅛ tsp grated nutmeg
salt and pepper to taste
2 cups water or beef stock
500 g spaghetti
½ cup grated parmesan cheese

Heat the oil in a large saucepan and sauté the onions and garlic until soft. Add the bacon and sauté for 1 minute. Add the beef and brown over high heat, stirring constantly to break up any lumps.

Add the tomatoes and their juices, tomato paste, herbs, nutmeg, salt and pepper and water or stock. Bring to the boil, then turn heat down and simmer for 40–60 minutes until most of the liquid has evaporated and sauce is thick.

Boil and drain the spaghetti and toss with a little butter. Pile into a serving bowl and sprinkle with half the cheese. Spoon over the bolognese sauce and serve with the remainder of the cheese.

Serves 6

Shepherd's Pie

Mum has an aversion to potatoes far beyond the realms of dislike. She cannot even be in the room while they are being cooked! So when I first tackled Shepherd's Pie in the kitchen at home she actually had to stand outside and supervise me from the window, making sure that I did not destroy the kitchen whilst she sheltered behind the glass. Here's our Shepherd's Pie—as supervised through the window!

olive oil, for frying
500 g minced lamb
salt and pepper
1 large onion, finely grated
1 large carrot, peeled and finely grated
2 cloves garlic
2 tbsp Worcestershire sauce
1 tbsp tomato paste

1 sprig rosemary, chopped
1 cup red wine
1¼ cups chicken stock
1 kg Royal Blue potatoes, peeled and cut into chunks
2 heaped tbsp butter
2 egg yolks
parmesan, for grating

Preheat the oven to 180°C.

Heat the oil in a large saucepan until hot. Season the mince with salt and pepper and fry in the oil over moderate to high heat for 2–3 minutes.

Stir the onions and carrot into the mince then grate the garlic in as well. Add the Worcestershire sauce, tomato paste and rosemary and cook for 1–2 minutes, stirring constantly. Pour in the red wine and reduce until it has almost completely evaporated. Add the chicken stock, bring to the boil and simmer until the sauce has thickened.

Meanwhile, cook the potatoes in boiling salted water until tender. Drain then return to the hot pan over low heat to dry out briefly. Pass them through a potato ricer (or mash them if you don't have one) then stir in the butter and beat in the egg yolks, followed by about 2 tablespoons of grated parmesan. Season.

Spoon the mince into the bottom of a large ovenproof dish. Using a large spoon, spread the mashed potato generously on top of the mince. Grate some parmesan over the top and season. Bake in the oven for approximately 20 minutes, until golden brown.

Serves 6

Max Walker and his mother, Dulcie Evelyn Walker

So many of my memories of my mum are centred around the kitchen table—laughing, loving and living life.

My mother adored cooking meals and loved nothing more than an empty plate as acknowledgement ... she always prepared enough to serve seconds.

Dulcie was a farm girl who collected hens' eggs at first light, milked the cows and walked fresh produce to market before school. Together with her Mum, they would make batches of butter. They'd create spontaneous meals from the pantry and garden paddock on a wood fire stove. The Institute of Experience.

When we lived in the Empire Hotel, Mum's cooking was a magnet for overnight guests. She would offer two serves of Pea and Ham Soup to the travelling salesmen ... they never ate much else, it was so good and so filling.

Every year she served up the perfect roast dinner for Christmas. Pudding spotted with three-penny and six-penny coins, the hot, yummy custard and ice-cream … I shut my eyes now and I can see, taste and smell the offerings. Never did break a tooth—merely topped up the money box and added to the memory bank.

My first overseas cricket tour was to the Caribbean. Every day we ate chicken (wild water fowl), or curried goat with fried rice and 25 different varieties of blowflies to add colour.

On my return three and a half months later, I vowed never to eat chicken again. Incredible how the sports circuit consisted of nothing but baked, steamed, barbecued or under-cooked chicken. But up stepped Mum with: 'I will make you something different, like you have never had before.'

Hypnotic Chook

❦

Somewhere along the line, between my hypnotising chooks in the backyard of the Empire Hotel and later publishing a book How to Hypnotise Chooks, *Mum took up the mantle and referred to her dish as a real, heart-felt Hypnotised Chook. It tended to make the eyes spin a little and the constitution concentrate ... a total gastronomic experience, unforgettable. Way to go, Ma.*

4 skinless chicken fillets, diced
2 garlic cloves, crushed
1-cm piece fresh ginger
3 tbsp soy sauce
½ lemon or lime, juiced
sesame oil, for frying
6 spring onions, cut to short
    lengths

1 red capsicum, sliced
1 handful bean shoots
small bunch bok choy
1 handful of snow peas, trimmed
egg noodles or rice, cooked as
    per packet instructions
chilli as desired

Marinate the chicken in the crushed garlic, ginger, soy sauce and lemon or lime juice. Set aside for 2 hours if possible. Drain marinade and reserve.

Cook the chicken in a little hot sesame oil in a hot wok, remove and set aside.

Heat a little more oil in the wok and add the chopped spring onions and capsicum. Stir fry quickly, add bean shoots, bok choy and snow peas a little later. When the snow peas are bright green, add the noodles, reserved marinade and chicken ... season to taste and add chilli if liked. Toss together to reheat and serve.

Serves 4

Apricot Steamed Pudding

For some years, Mum was the 'Master Chef' for a women's private hospital in Carlton ... variety and taste rolled out of the kitchen every day. Her Roly-poly Pudding was to die for, so too was the apricot jam pudding, steam-cooked!

melted butter for greasing the pudding basin
125 g butter, at room temperature
½ cup caster sugar
2 tsp pure vanilla
2 eggs

1 cup diced dried apricots
¾ cup milk
1½ cups self-raising flour
½ cup plain flour
1 cup apricot jam
¼ cup water

Brush a 6-cup capacity pudding basin with melted butter. Refrigerate for 5 minutes. Brush again with melted butter and line the basin with baking paper.

Beat the butter, sugar and vanilla with an electric mixer until light and creamy. Add the eggs, one at time, beating well after each addition. Transfer the mixture to a large bowl.

Stir in the apricots. Add the milk and flours, alternately, folding until well combined. Spoon the mixture into the pudding basin. Cover with baking paper, then foil. Secure with string.

Place the pudding basin on top of a trivet or upside-down saucer in a large saucepan. Fill the pan with boiling water until it is two-thirds up the sides of the basin. Simmer for 2 hours.

Stir jam and water in a saucepan over low heat until simmering and well combined. Sieve mixture until smooth.

Remove pudding from saucepan, invert onto a serving plate, spoon over warm jam and serve immediately.

Serves 4

Acknowledgements

Recipes My Mother Cooked wouldn't have been possible without the goodwill of the wonderful contributors who generously gave us their favourite recipes and recalled their precious childhood memories.

We are delighted to have such a talented and diverse group of people together in one place and we hope their recipes will inspire you to spend time with your family, cooking, eating and enjoying life together.

Sincere thanks to everyone that follows:

Robyn Archer is a singer, writer, director, and public advocate of the arts. She is Creative Director of the Canberra Centenary 2013.

Chef and author **Anil Ashokan** is the owner of Qmin, one of Sydney's leading Indian restaurants.

Maggie Beer is a South Australian cook, food author, restaurateur and food manufacturer. Her TV series 'The Cook and the Chef' (with Simon Bryant) ran for four years and is now available on DVD. Maggie was named Senior Australian of the Year for 2010.

Allan Campion is a food writer who operates 'foodies' tours and cooking classes around Melbourne.

Cheong Liew was the first Australian chef to be awarded an OAM for his culinary influence. The Liew family food philosophy was to 'live to eat' as distinct from 'eat to live'.

Vic Cherikoff is the leading authority on Australian wild foods and medicines and developing their uses as functional ingredients in foods, beverages, nutraceuticals and cosmetics.

Jill Dupleix is a food writer for *Epicure*, *Good Living* and *delicious* and is author of 15 cookbooks.

The owner of Lucio's, **Lucio Galletto** OAM, has been serving sophisticated Italian food to Sydney's media and political heavyweights and artists (whose work lines the walls) for over 25 years.

Gabriel Gaté is a chef with an international reputation as a cookery author, television presenter and cookery teacher.

Spice merchant **Ian Hemphill** is owner (with wife Liz) of Herbie's Spices, and an author, TV and radio presenter, spice appreciation class tutor and spice tour leader.

Alex Herbert is co-owner and chef of Bird Cow Fish in Surry Hills, Sydney.

Iain 'Huey' Hewitson is a restaurateur and author of many books, and has been a TV chef for 19 years.

Peter Kuruvita is co-owner of Flying Fish restaurant in Sydney, and also owns Flying Fish Fiji in the Sheraton Denarau. He is a restaurant consultant and author of *Serendip: My Sri Lankan Kitchen*.

Editorial consultant **Carolyn Lockhart** is the former editor of *Vogue Entertaining*, *Australian Gourmet Traveller* and the Qantas inflight magazine.

Kate McGhie has made a career out of cooking and writing about food. Her weekly column in Melbourne's *Herald Sun* reaches some 1.5 million readers.

Joanna McMillan Price is a registered nutritionist, accredited practising dietitian and media health commentator and presenter.

Stefano Manfredi has been a chef and restaurateur for over 25 years and has written about food for almost as long.

Lyndey Milan is a multi-award-winning food and wine communicator, television personality, cookbook author, restaurant reviewer and an ambassador for the Breast Cancer Network Australia.

Roberta Muir manages Sydney Seafood School, reviews restaurants, judges cheese and writes about food, wine and travel.

Freelance journalist and author **John Newton** writes on food, eating, travel, farming and associated environmental issues.

Chef **Armando Percuoco** has worked in restaurants most of his life. His Buon Ricordo is a landmark of the Sydney dining scene.

Damien Pignolet is executive chef and co-owner of Sydney restaurant Bistro Moncur and has been an influential teacher of cookery for more than three decades.

Food writer and author **Jan Purser** is also a naturopathic nutritionist, health writer, corporate health educator and artist.

Cherry Ripe is an award-winning food writer, journalist, broadcaster and author of five books. She writes for *The Australian* and has contributed to *The Observer* (UK) and *The Wall Street Journal* (US).

Writer **Philippa Sandall** is editor of the online food and health newsletter *GI News* and creator of the best-selling 'New Glucose Revolution' series with Sydney University's Prof Jennie Brand-Miller.

Joanna Savill is director of the Sydney International Food Festival, co-editor of the SMH *Good Food Guide* and co-creator of *The Food Lovers' Guide to Australia* TV series.

Catherine Saxelby is a nutritionist, 'foodologist' and founder of the popular Foodwatch website. She eats, drinks, tastes, tests, tweets and blogs about food, diet and nutrition.

Steven Snow is chef and owner of the award-winning seafood restaurant Fins, in Kingscliff. He is regularly interviewed on ABC radio, presents a cooking segment on Guide to the Good Life on Channel 7 and has published a cookbook.

Food writer and educator **Kathy Snowball** teaches at Sydney Seafood School, tends her garden in Orange and edits 'taste O', the *Central Western Daily*'s monthly food and wine supplement.

Charmaine Solomon OAM is an internationally acclaimed and best-selling cookery author with a range of gourmet curry pastes, marinades and spice blends marketed under the Charmaine's Kitchen brand.

Deborah Solomon's interest in food was well established early in life thanks to her mother, Charmaine. She has worked in the food industry as a chef, and developed recipes for magazines.

Deborah Solomon's daughter, **Jenna Hand**, is a Canberra journalist who shares the family passion for creating and sharing good food.

Chef **Craig Squire** runs Ochre Restaurant—a highly awarded Cairns restaurant specialising in local seafood, game, bush foods and regional Australian cuisine.

Brisbane's Buffalo Club chef **Ryan Squires** was voted Australia's best new talent in the *Australian Gourmet Traveller* 2010 awards.

Chef **Tony Tan** is a cooking school owner and Asian food lover. He is creative director (cultural) of the Melbourne Food & Wine Festival.

Comedian **Josh Thomas** was the youngest ever winner of the Melbourne International Comedy Festival's RAW Comedy Competition (at 17). He competed in 2009's *Celebrity MasterChef*.

Chef **Hadleigh Troy**'s Restaurant Amusé was awarded Two Stars and rated the number one restaurant in Western Australia by *Australian Gourmet Traveller* in 2009.

Former Australian test cricketer and VFL/AFL footballer **Max Walker** is an entrepreneur, media personality and motivational speaker who has written 14 books.

Thanks also to the McGrath Foundation, who have been an inspiring partner to work with. In particular, thanks to Kylea Tink for making it happen.

Index